P9-APG-321

OPPOSING VIEWPOINTS®

HUMANITY'S
FUTURE

Other Books of Related Interest

OPPOSING VIEWPOINTS®

HUMANITY'S FUTURE

Louise I. Gerdes, *Book Editor*

Bonnie Szumski, *Publisher*
Helen Cothran, *Managing Editor*

**OPPOSING
VIEWPOINTS®
SERIES**

GREENHAVEN PRESS
An imprint of Thomson Gale, a part of The Thomson Corporation

THOMSON
———————✦———————™
GALE

Detroit • New York • San Francisco • San Diego • New Haven, Conn.
Waterville, Maine • London • Munich

LIBRARY OF CONGRESS CATALOGING-IN-PUBLICATION DATA
Humanity's future / Louise I. Gerdes, book editor.
p. cm. — (Opposing viewpoints series)
Includes bibliographical references and index.
ISBN 0-7377-2939-2 (lib. : alk. paper) — ISBN 0-7377-2940-6 (pbk. : alk. paper)
1. Technology—Social aspects—Forecasting. 2. Twenty-first century—Forecasts.
I. Gerdes, Louise I., 1953– . II. Opposing viewpoints series (Unnumbered)
T14.5.H865 2006
303.48'3—dc22   2005042446

Printed in the United States of America

"Congress shall make no law... abridging the freedom of speech, or of the press."

First Amendment to the U.S. Constitution

The basic foundation of our democracy is the First Amendment guarantee of freedom of expression. The Opposing Viewpoints Series is dedicated to the concept of this basic freedom and the idea that it is more important to practice it than to enshrine it.

Contents

Why Consider Opposing Viewpoints?

"The only way in which a human being can make some approach to knowing the whole of a subject is by hearing what can be said about it by persons of every variety of opinion and studying all modes in which it can be looked at by every character of mind. No wise man ever acquired his wisdom in any mode but this."

John Stuart Mill

In our media-intensive culture it is not difficult to find differing opinions. Thousands of newspapers and magazines and dozens of radio and television talk shows resound with differing points of view. The difficulty lies in deciding which opinion to agree with and which "experts" seem the most credible. The more inundated we become with differing opinions and claims, the more essential it is to hone critical reading and thinking skills to evaluate these ideas. Opposing Viewpoints books address this problem directly by presenting stimulating debates that can be used to enhance and teach these skills. The varied opinions contained in each book examine many different aspects of a single issue. While examining these conveniently edited opposing views, readers can develop critical thinking skills such as the ability to compare and contrast authors' credibility, facts, argumentation styles, use of persuasive techniques, and other stylistic tools. In short, the Opposing Viewpoints Series is an ideal way to attain the higher-level thinking and reading skills so essential in a culture of diverse and contradictory opinions.

In addition to providing a tool for critical thinking, Opposing Viewpoints books challenge readers to question their own strongly held opinions and assumptions. Most people form their opinions on the basis of upbringing, peer pressure, and personal, cultural, or professional bias. By reading carefully balanced opposing views, readers must directly confront new ideas as well as the opinions of those with whom they disagree. This is not to simplistically argue that everyone who reads opposing views will—or should—change his or her opinion. Instead, the series enhances readers' understanding of their own views by encouraging confrontation with opposing ideas. Careful examination of others' views can lead to the readers' understanding of the logical inconsistencies in their own opinions, perspective on why they hold an opinion, and the consideration of the possibility that their opinion requires further evaluation.

Evaluating Other Opinions

To ensure that this type of examination occurs, Opposing Viewpoints books present all types of opinions. Prominent spokespeople on different sides of each issue as well as well-known professionals from many disciplines challenge the reader. An additional goal of the series is to provide a forum for other, less known, or even unpopular viewpoints. The opinion of an ordinary person who has had to make the decision to cut off life support from a terminally ill relative, for example, may be just as valuable and provide just as much insight as a medical ethicist's professional opinion. The editors have two additional purposes in including these less known views. One, the editors encourage readers to respect others' opinions—even when not enhanced by professional credibility. It is only by reading or listening to and objectively evaluating others' ideas that one can determine whether they are worthy of consideration. Two, the inclusion of such viewpoints encourages the important critical thinking skill of objectively evaluating an author's credentials and bias. This evaluation will illuminate an author's reasons for taking a particular stance on an issue and will aid in readers' evaluation of the author's ideas.

It is our hope that these books will give readers a deeper understanding of the issues debated and an appreciation of the complexity of even seemingly simple issues when good and honest people disagree. This awareness is particularly important in a democratic society such as ours in which people enter into public debate to determine the common good. Those with whom one disagrees should not be regarded as enemies but rather as people whose views deserve careful examination and may shed light on one's own.

Thomas Jefferson once said that "difference of opinion leads to inquiry, and inquiry to truth." Jefferson, a broadly educated man, argued that "if a nation expects to be ignorant and free . . . it expects what never was and never will be." As individuals and as a nation, it is imperative that we consider the opinions of others and examine them with skill and discernment. The Opposing Viewpoints Series is intended to help readers achieve this goal.

David L. Bender and Bruno Leone,
Founders

Introduction

"If we look ahead a few decades, we note that our civilization has enormous potential, not only to flourish happily but also to deteriorate appallingly. . . . Humanity's future is not predetermined, preordained, nor carved in granite. On the grand scale of some ancient cosmic myth, our worldwide civilization today is engaged in a titanic struggle."

Excerpt from Crucial Questions About the Future by Allen Tough, social scientist, educator, and futurist.

Despite technology's central role in humanity's evolution, there have always been people who have viewed advances in technology as a threat to humanity's future. These attitudes have in some cases led to bans on these advances. For example, when in 1734 French philosopher Voltaire argued for experimental inoculation against smallpox, his request was ultimately denied due to fears about technology's effects on humanity. According to historian Alan Charles Kors, Voltaire asked French leaders to consider "the benefits to be gained by applying our knowledge of nature to the knowable and remediable causes of human suffering." In response, the French government consulted two well-respected authorities at the University of Paris: the Faculty of Medicine and the Faculty of Theology. According to Kors, the Faculty of Medicine believed that "[inoculation] would take us into uncharted and dangerous seas of innovation beyond the control of rightful authority. It would vitiate the sorts of traditions that had kept us decent and humane." The Faculty of Theology argued that inoculation was an attempt to play God. For them, Kors explains, "inoculation was an act of hubris, a wanton and insolent human intrusion on God's domain, and if we crossed that line, how would we ever find our way back to our rightful place in the natural order?" As a result of these views, inoculating people against smallpox remained a crime in France until King Louis XV died of the disease on May 10, 1774. Such debates over technology still occur today. Although technological advances are not the only factors shaping humanity's future, technology has had and will continue to have an enormous impact on people throughout the world.

Those who comment on the impact of technology on humanity's future generally fall into two camps. While some are confident that technology will solve any problems humanity may face, others are less optimistic about its potential to solve increasingly complex problems. Those who are confident about humanity's future often recommend public policies that encourage the vigorous pursuit of technology. Those who feel the unrestricted pursuit of technology poses a threat to humanity's future often prefer policies that limit, and sometimes ban, the pursuit of some technologies.

The controversy over therapeutic cloning illustrates this division. This biomedical technique involves the transplantation of the nuclei of a patient's cells into embryonic cells, which are then stimulated to reproduce, creating an embryo that is an exact genetic copy of the patient. The goal of creating this embryo is that it might then be used to create healthy cells to replace unhealthy ones in patients that suffer from debilitating diseases such as Alzheimer's, diabetes, and Parkinson's. Therapeutic cloning is thus distinguished from reproductive cloning, the goal of which is to create a human baby. Some view therapeutic cloning as a miraculous process that could help millions who suffer from debilitating diseases. Because of their belief in therapeutic cloning's potential to improve humanity's future, supporters contend that research should be pursued with little restriction. Others fear that therapeutic cloning could too easily lead to reproductive cloning and should therefore be banned.

The arguments made by opponents of therapeutic cloning are representative of those who believe that some technologies pose a threat to humanity's future. Therapeutic cloning, they argue, is immoral and threatens human rights. Cloning human embryos simply to destroy them for medical research is abhorrent, in their view. "The embryo, however created and however small, is a human being and therefore should be granted the rights and protections of a human being," asserts law and medical ethics professor R. Alto Charo.

To prevent abuses, Leon R. Kass, chairman of the President's Council on Bioethics, argues that therapeutic cloning should be banned. Kass contends that allowing cloned embryos to be produced for biomedical research and/or stem cell extraction is morally highly problematic. It crosses several important moral boundaries that in his view accelerates our slide down a slippery slope into a dehumanizing world of genetic control of offspring and the routine use of nascent human life as a mere natural resource. Laws have in fact been proposed that make it a crime to use any form of human cloning, including therapeutic cloning. The Human Cloning Prohibition Act of 2001, which, as of June 2005, has yet to be approved, would make all forms of cloning a crime. Under the act anyone who performs a human cloning can be imprisoned for up to ten years. Moreover, if the cloning was conducted for "pecuniary gain," participants could pay a fine of not less than $1 million.

Those who support therapeutic cloning object to such laws. According to Paul Berg, who won the Nobel Prize in chemistry for his work on recombinant DNA, "Criminalizing pure science is an absurd throwback to prohibitions on speaking out on scientific issues or new truths." The arguments posed by Berg and others who support therapeutic cloning are representative of those who believe that technology will improve humanity's future. According to Kors, if the government criminalizes biomedical research such as therapeutic cloning, "we have criminalized the effort both to understand nature and to make that knowledge available to those who choose to use it voluntarily and peacefully. We have criminalized the pursuit of knowledge that could alleviate human agony." Moreover, these analysts argue, policies could protect against abuses. Berg argues, "A process resembling the one . . . instituted to oversee gene therapy experimentation could be implemented to ensure that [therapeutic cloning] technology is done only to advance medical knowledge and develop medical therapies, and not for procreation."

The debate over therapeutic cloning's impact on humanity's future is ongoing. Like many of the authors in this anthology, supporters are optimistic while opponents are more pessimistic about the impact of technology on humanity. The authors in this volume explore the impact of technology and other issues concerning the future of humanity in the following chapters of *Opposing Viewpoints: Humanity's Future:* How Will Technology Affect Humanity's Future? What Is the Future of World Health? How Will the Human Impact on the Environment Affect Humanity's Future? What Will Be the Future of the Global Community? Whether these authors' predictions about humanity's future will be realized remains to be seen.

CHAPTER 1

How Will Technology Affect Humanity's Future?

Chapter Preface

In the future, some commentators claim, people will be able to create anything they want with the help of self-replicating nanoassemblers. "Shovel in some dirt and out would pop a computer, a car, a pair of khakis, or a cabbage, depending on the recipe you specified," maintains writer Ronald Bailey. This is the future foreseen by nanotechnology visionaries. Nanotechnology is the science of manipulating inorganic materials at the atomic or molecular level to create materials or simple machines. Since a nanometer is one-billionth of a meter, these materials and machines are extremely small. Although people cannot yet create a pair of jeans simply by manipulating dirt, nanotechnology is already being used in consumer products such as wrinkle- and stain-free pants. The technology has generated debate, however, which is representative of many debates over technology's effect on humanity's future.

Proponents see nanotechnology as revolutionary. "The impact of this is going to be as great, if not greater, than the steam engine or the computer," claims Julie Chen, a National Science Foundation (NSF) program director. "People are going to look back and see it as another Industrial Revolution," she maintains. Experts predict that nanotechnology will eliminate the world's dependence on oil. They also envision products such as self-repairing highways and ingestible particles that attack cancer cells.

However, everyone does not share this enthusiasm. Some scientists fear the consequences of this unproven technology. Nanotechnology opponents argue that research should be halted until the technology is proven to pose no threat to the environment and human health. An oft-cited opponent of nanotechnology, Sun Microsystems cofounder Bill Joy, fears what has come to be known as the "gray goo" problem. Because natural life forms could not compete with intelligent, self-replicating nanomachines, Joy argues, these machines could eventually cover the planet, wiping out all life. The earth's biomass would then turn into a gray goo. Joy maintains that his concerns come directly from nanotechnology visionary MIT engineer K. Eric Drexler. While Drexler believed that nanotechnology could be controlled, his vision, in Joy's view, is frightening. In his book *Engines of Creation*, Drexler explains:

[Nanotech] "Plants" with "leaves" no more efficient than today's solar cells could out-compete real plants, crowding the biosphere with an inedible foliage. Tough omnivorous "bacteria" could out-compete real bacteria: They could spread like blowing pollen, replicate swiftly, and reduce the biosphere to dust in a matter of days. Dangerous replicators could easily be too tough, small, and rapidly spreading to stop—at least if we make no preparation.

Joy proposes that nanotech research should be suspended. "It would seem worthwhile to question whether we need to take such a high risk of total destruction to gain yet more knowledge and yet more things; common sense says that there is a limit to our material needs—and that certain knowledge is too dangerous and is best forgone."

Nanotech proponents contend that such claims are unwarranted. "This idea of nanobots multiplying into infinity is not realistic," argues Mihail C. Roco, a senior adviser for nanotechnology at the NSF. The nature of nanotech products, proponents contend, preclude such a scenario. "With most new things, like tennis rackets or clothes, the nanoparticles are embedded in the product," maintains Christine Peterson, cofounder and president of the Foresight Institute, a nanotech think tank in Palo Alto, California. "So this idea that you have all these loose molecules all over the place is simply not true," she asserts. Nanotech industry representatives agree. "Of course, there are safety concerns, as in any industry, and we should address them," says Lynn E. Foster, a Los Angeles nanotechnology analyst. "But there is nothing here that warrants a moratorium," Foster maintains.

Whether nanotechnology poses a threat or will prove to be a great benefit to humanity remains controversial. The viewpoints expressed by opponents and proponents in the nanotechnology debate—whether to exercise restraint or earnestly push on developing new technologies—are representative of those expressed by some of the authors in the following chapter. Nanotech opponent Bill Joy concedes that the question of how technology will affect humanity's future is unknown. He writes, "Whether we are to succeed or fail, to survive or fall victim to these technologies, is not yet decided."

"Humanity's activities, including the entire scientific and technological enterprise, represent a unified attempt . . . to spread 'humanness' to everything we encounter."

Technology Will Enhance Humanity's Future

Michael G. Zey

According to Michael G. Zey in the following viewpoint, humanity is destined to control and transform the universe to its benefit. For example, humanity will eradicate poverty by manufacturing food using nanotechnology, asserts Zey. Humanity also will achieve total unity, he claims, by building a transportation, communication, and power grid that all will share. Moreover, to achieve its goals and extend human life, humanity will enhance the human body with genetic engineering and robotics, he asserts. Zey is executive director of the Expansionary Institute, a research organization that focuses on future trends.

As you read, consider the following questions:
1. According to Zey, how does dominionization help humanity vitalize the planet and universe?
2. How does species coalescence empower humanity to achieve the author's vision of vitalization?
3. In the author's opinion, what is the ultimate determinant of the shape and direction of the universe?

As we humans evolve, we increase our power over nature and our own destiny. The next step of human progress will be to inhabit, enhance, and eventually transform the universe. . . .

Over the past few years, the rate of human achievement in all scientific fields has accelerated dramatically. We are transforming the human body; tinkering with our genetic arrangement to make ourselves smarter, faster, and healthier; and then developing ways to clone the final product. We enhance the functioning of the brain and implant that human brainpower into our machines. And we unify the human family by developing global communication systems, such as the Internet.

As our species extends our control over this planet, we simultaneously prepare ourselves for extraterrestrial habitation by shaping and transforming terrestrial landscapes. We design a new generation of rockets that can transport us to distant spheres at one-third the speed of light. At the same time, we probe the innermost recesses of nature through such exotic fields as nanotechnology.

The Imperative to Progress

We must examine the many ways such developments impact the individual, society, and the economy. And we must explore the underlying reasons why our species is feverishly working to advance the planet and ourselves and transform all we encounter. When we truly understand the depth and strength of man's overwhelming imperative to grow and progress, we can more clearly anticipate the future.

At first blush, it would seem that there is little mystery about the impulses driving the human species in this quest: We engage in such productive activities merely to enhance our material condition. We invent technologies that will improve our standard of living and make our lives more pleasant and comfortable. Our species from the earliest periods of prehistory seems compelled not just to survive, but to grow, progress, and enhance itself and its environment. At each new level of our development, we endeavor to master our environment as well as the physical dynamics governing our universe.

Humanity's activities, including the entire scientific and

technological enterprise, represent a unified attempt by the species to spread "humanness" to everything we encounter. Over the centuries, we have labored to improve planet Earth, and we are now preparing to transform the universe into a dynamic entity filled with life. We will accomplish this by extending our consciousness, skills, intellect, and our very selves to other spheres.

I label the sum total of our species' endeavors to improve and change our planetary environment—and ultimately the universe itself—vitalization. Vitalization is a force that is conditioning human behavior. The drive to vitalize—to imbue our planet and eventually the cosmos with a consciousness and intelligence—is a primary motivation behind all human productive activity.

Toward a Vitalized Universe

Vitalization is the primary force shaping human behavior. However, in order to pursue vitalization successfully, the human species must master four other forces, what I label the "building blocks of vitalization." These four processes encompass the extraordinary advances in areas such as space, medicine, biogenetics, engineering, cybernetics, and energy.

The four supporting forces are:

- Dominionization: control over physical forces, such as energy.
- Species coalescence: unity through built systems, such as transportation and communications.
- Biogenesis: improvement of the physical shell, such as through bioengineering.
- Cybergenesis: interconnection with machines to advance human evolution.

Each of these forces plays a critical catalytic role in the achievement of vitalization.

Dominionization: Controlling Nature

The term *dominionization* refers to the process whereby humankind establishes control over several key aspects of its physical universe. With each passing decade, we enhance our ability to manipulate matter, reshape the planet, develop innovative energy sources, and control fundamental aspects of the physical universe, such as the atom and electromagnetism. Someday, we will learn to influence weather patterns and climate.

In a host of ways, dominionization helps humanity vitalize the planet and eventually the universe. As we master the basic dynamics of nature, we are more able to shepherd the evolution of our planet as well as others. As we develop novel and powerful forms of energy, we can rocket from one sphere to another. Moreover, by improving our already formidable skills in moving mountains and creating lakes, we will be better able to change both the topography and the geography of other planets.

Shaping the Future

The future will be shaped by the renovations and advances of the present: by what we develop, what we build, what we learn, what we discover, what we try and test and deem worthwhile. Progress, in this sense, is made possible by improvements in our knowledge and understanding, our abilities, our circumstances, our institutions, our technology, and our control over nature and chance. There is of course always a danger that we may misuse our newfound powers, or even that they might corrupt us; but there are also reasons to believe that we will learn to use them responsibly, and that they will enhance our lives and improve our world. Armed with a sense of the potential pitfalls, we stand a good chance of using our new technologies well.

Yuval Levin, *New Atlantis*, Winter 2004.

Examples of dominionization abound. Major macroengineering projects attest to man's ability to transform the very surface of the earth. By constructing man-made lakes, we will be able to live in previously uninhabitable areas such as interior Australia. Shimizu Corporation envisions a subterranean development called Urban Geo Grid—a series of cities linked by tunnels—accommodating half a million people. In the emerging Macroindustrial Era, whose framework was established in the 1970s and 1980s, we will redefine the concept of "bigness" as we dot Earth's landscape with immense architectural structures. Takenaka, a Japanese construction firm, has proposed "Sky City 1000," a 3,000-foot tower, to be built in

Tokyo. Another firm, Ohbayashi, plans to erect a 500-story high-rise building featuring apartments, offices, shopping centers, and service facilities.

We will establish dominion over the very heart of physical matter itself. Through nanotechnology, our species will attain control over the atom and its tiniest components. Such control will enable us to effortlessly "macromanufacture" from the bottom up, one atom at a time, any material object. This will enable us to permanently eradicate age-old problems such as scarcity and poverty.

We will also establish dominion over our physical realm by mastering the energy production process. We are on the verge of developing a cheap, accessible form of nuclear fusion for general use, and various companies and government agencies are seriously experimenting with exotic phenomena such as electromagnetism to explore its possible application to energy production.

We will travel to the Moon, planets, and asteroids to mine exotic new forms of energy. Organizations such as the Space Studies Institute in Princeton, New Jersey, are drawing up the blueprints for a Solar Power Satellite that will sit in geostationary orbit above the equator, collect cheap and abundant solar energy, and beam it down to Earth in microwave form for land-based energy production and consumption.

Species Coalescence: United We Progress

In the Macroindustrial Era, humanity will also pursue another process critical to the achievement of vitalization. Species coalescence refers to the sequence through which humanity achieves total unity—physically, culturally, and functionally.

Species coalescence empowers us to achieve vitalization in a number of ways. On the purely functional level, such coalescence makes it more likely that all members and groups across the globe will work together, pooling their diverse skills and talents, to facilitate the vitalization process. In addition, coalescence enables us to develop a sense of membership in a common human family, not unlike the sense of common identity shared by members of a clan, village, or a neighborhood community.

Mankind is accelerating species coalescence through the development of a global transportation grid, the universal communications network, and other mechanisms. The global transportation grid includes the hyperplane, which promises to reduce the New York-to-Tokyo trip to two hours; smart roads to speed automobiles; and supertunnels such as the Chunnel. Construction of a global high-speed rail system will prove crucial to the achievement of species coalescence. In 1998, the United States finally passed legislation that would release millions of dollars for the development of a magnetic levitation train line. Construction of such a 310-mile-per-hour train could begin as early as [2001].

Governments and corporations are partnering in the construction of a global power grid that would link Europe, North America, and Asia. With this grid in operation, Siberia could send power to North America over a link across the Bering Strait. In addition, a number of tunnel, bridge, and causeway projects will accelerate the species coalescence process. A Gibraltar crossing may soon connect Europe and Africa. Moreover, various countries are still planning to build within the decade the proposed Bering Strait crossing, which would link Asia and North America.

The universal communication network of images, voice, and data is made possible by satellites, fiber optics, and other advanced technologies. The Internet, still in its infancy, is only a harbinger of things to come. Hastening this societal convergence is the fact that previously unconnected nations and communities are becoming integrated into the worldwide production-consumption web as manufacturers, designers, inventors, and consumers.

Biogenesis: Advancing Human Evolution

These remarkable triumphs of human ingenuity represent only part of the process by which humanity is vitalizing the cosmos. As we enter the next century, humanity is feverishly working toward assuming control of its very physical development and long-term evolutionary advancement. I label this process biogenesis: the modification, enhancement, and in some cases transformation of the human body.

To achieve vitalization we must assume control over our

physical selves. Vitalization will require an "enhanced" version of the human being—smarter, more adroit, more creative. Through such techniques as genetic manipulation, cloning, and other forms of physical reconfiguring of the body, we will create that "new and improved" human. Moreover, since we will be traveling to other planets and distant galaxies, we must learn how to modify the body, adapt it to these different environments. Also, protracted processes such as vitalization require human physical beings that are durable; they must live decades or centuries longer than they do now.

We will achieve biogenesis by developing a host of new technologies. Scientists at the Geron Corporation and the University of Colorado at Boulder claim they have found the immortality gene, the gene that controls the aging process in humans. They boast that, by tinkering with this gene, they soon might be able to equip the human body with a set of instructions to simply stop aging.

The magical new science of nanotechnology will allow us to shape and redesign the human body as we see fit. It opens the possibility of creating wholly new organs to help us adapt to new environments. We might even develop nanomachines that cruise through a patient's body and fight viruses, including HIV/AIDS. Companies such as Advanced Tissue Sciences Inc. and Organogenesis have developed tissue regeneration and tissue-engineering techniques that will make the body resistant to diseases such as Alzheimer's and cystic fibrosis, and could help the body regenerate missing parts. Another development, cloning, will allow us to replicate body types resistant to diseases and adaptable to a variety of environments (including outer space).

Bionics will also further species development. Researchers in the United States, at Johns Hopkins University and the University of North Carolina at Chapel Hill, as well as those in Japan are working on an artificial retina that will allow blind persons to be able to detect motion and light and eventually experience simulated sight.

Cybergenesis: Sing the Body Electronic

Throughout the twenty-first century, humanity will engage in another process crucial to its advancement. Cybergenesis refers to the incorporation of computers, microchips, and cybernetics into the human evolution process. Robotics, and automation in general, will enhance the functioning of the human brain. The computer will contribute to the human species' growth and development by enhancing the brain's functioning, as a surrogate memory, visualizer, calculator, and decision maker.

To the extent that it makes us smarter, and hence more adaptable, cybernetics becomes an integral part of our achievement of vitalization. Cybergenesis will imbue the species with the brainpower and mental dexterity to perform the computational and conceptual feats required to vitalize planets, including our own.

Soon, nanocomputers will be placed inside the brains of humans to enhance memory, thinking ability, visualization, and general sensing. Researchers at British Telecommunications PLC [a British publicly held corporation] seek to develop a computer that can be implanted in the brain to complement human memory and computational skill. In addition, technologies are at hand that will enable the human brain to "connect" to a computer and download and upload data.

Brain science researchers are revealing how technology can help us expand humans' physical and mental abilities and powers. At such sites as the Yale/Veterans Affairs PET [positron emission tomography] Center in West Haven, Connecticut, scientists are diligently developing ways for an amputee's brain to redesign itself and grow new communication paths to reattached limbs. The U.S. government senses the importance of such research into cognitive functioning. In the 1990s, Congress authorized the "Human Brain," a joint effort of NASA [National Aeronautics and Space Administration], the National Institute of Mental Health, the National Institute on Aging, the National Science Foundation, and the Office of Naval Research. This project's purpose is to develop technology to alter and improve the operation of the human brain and enlarge people's brain capacity, thereby furthering the process of cybergenesis.

By its very definition, vitalization involves the transference of organic life and human consciousness to other spheres throughout the universe. Therefore, we must examine the role that space exploration and colonization play in both the evolution of humanity and the ultimate development and perfection of the universe. Through space exploration and travel we will fundamentally redefine ourselves, from Earth-bound to "extraterrestrial." At that point, we will become active participants in the development of the universe as we spread human consciousness and organic life itself throughout a currently dead universe. Vitalization will also be achieved through terraformation, the creation of organic environments on Mars and other barren spheres. This process is being enabled by pioneering work performed by the Engineering Society for Advancing Mobility (SAE) and the Millennial Projects, as well as bold new efforts by countries such as China, Japan, and the United States, to colonize planets and vitalize these spheres' terrestrial and climatic environments.

An Emerging Vision of a Truly Human Future

Our species is guided by a sense of higher purpose, a destiny, as it were, of which we are only now becoming aware. This new vision synthesizes a century of scientific and theoretic research into the nature of the human species and our ultimate place and role in the evolving universe.

The emergence of human consciousness and human intelligence is a unique historical event—the human race's capacity to vitalize, bring life, order, creativity, and novelty to everything it touches, sets the world on a completely new evolutionary trajectory. Moreover, the world now possesses an entity, the human species, that could develop tools to save the universe from the Big Chill or the Big Crunch, the demise augured by the Big Bang theory.

Hence, human will is the ultimate determinant of the shape and direction of the universe. It will not be left to the universe to determine its ultimate fate—it has no concept of where it is going. At best, it will settle into a moribund chaos, at worst it will teeter on the edge of dissolution and destruction. The human being has a different destiny in mind for the cosmos—we are actively engaged in creating a Humaniverse of our own.

Such ruminations are hardly esoteric or "philosophical." Government and business leaders, if they are to make correct long- and short-term decisions regarding technological development and the economy, must understand the powerful role that the human species will play in the future. Indeed, speculation about such "cosmic" issues is becoming commonplace. Scientific discoveries by the Hubble Space Telescope and the Mars Pathfinder mission only fuel the debate over the place of man in the cosmos. Moreover, NASA has created an Astrobiology Program to study the origin, evolution, distribution, and purpose of life in the universe.

This new vision provides startling answers to the questions: Why us? Why here? Why now?

We are entering a human future, in which the very shape and direction of all aspects of the universe will be deeply influenced by the actions of the human race and its descendants. For example, the proposed terraformation of Mars—the creation of an earthlike environment on the Red Planet—encompasses more than a planetary facelift. It will represent a thorough "humanization" of that currently lifeless sphere.

The vitalized future will be a humane future, reflective of our core values—growth, progress, optimism, hope, and altruism. The very act of vitalization, the bringing of life to other worlds, implies that we are acting through exclusively human values—the desire to improve our surroundings, to enrich, embellish, and make the world a better place. While human imagination and energy will build this new world, our values will shape it.

We are now about to begin a journey into the future, to be challenged in ways we have never imagined. Let the adventure begin!

| *"Technologies and their uses should be limited and controlled by biblical ethics, not by our desires for more power or wealth."*

Technological Innovation Must Be Limited to Protect Humanity

Don Closson

The unquestioned pursuit of technology could have unintended adverse consequences and should therefore be limited, argues Don Closson in the following viewpoint. Many enlightened voices warn of the dangers of robotics, genetic engineering, and nanotechnology, Closson claims. Self-replicating nanotech weapons, he asserts, could destroy all plant life. Genetic engineering could result in a race of super-humans, ushering in a new era of inequality. To prevent the misuse of technology, he contends, humanity must resist the temptation to use technology to usurp dominion over God's kingdom. Closson is a research associate with Probe Ministries, an organization that promotes a Christian worldview.

As you read, consider the following questions:
1. In Closson's opinion, why is it easy for baby-boomers to discount apocalyptic language?
2. What kind of people is history full of, according to the author?
3. According to the author, with what have Christians everywhere had to struggle?

Don Closson, "Does the Future Need Us? The Future of Humanity and Technology," www.probe.org, 2002. Copyright © 2002 by Probe Ministries. Reproduced by permission.

In April of 2000, Bill Joy ignited a heated discussion concerning the role of technology in modern society. His article in *Wired* magazine became the focus of a growing concern that technological advances are coming so quickly and are so dramatic that they threaten the future existence of humanity itself. It is relatively easy for baby-boomers to discount such apocalyptic language since we grew up being entertained by countless movies and books warning of the dire consequences from uncontrolled scientific experimentation. We tend to lump cries of impending doom from technology with fringe lunatics like Ted Kaczynski, the Unabomber. Kaczynski killed three people and injured others in a seventeen-year attempt to scare away or kill researchers who were close to creating technologies that he felt might have unintended consequences.

Warning Voices

But Bill Joy is no Ted Kaczynski. He is the chief scientist for Sun Microsystems, a major player in computer technology and the Internet. He played an important role in the founding of Sun Microsystems and has been instrumental in making UNIX (operating system) the backbone of the Internet. So it is a surprise to find him warning us that some types of knowledge, some technologies should remain unexplored. Joy is calling for a new set of ethics that will guide our quest for knowledge away from dangerous research.

Another voice with a similar warning is that of Francis Fukuyama, professor of political economy at Johns Hopkins University. His book *Our Posthuman Future* asks disturbing questions about the potential unintended results from the current revolution in biotechnology. He writes, "the most significant threat posed by contemporary biotechnology is the possibility that it will alter human nature and thereby move us into a 'posthuman' stage of history." Once human nature is disrupted, the belief that we are created equal might no longer be tenable causing both civil and economic strife.

There is also a Christian tradition that questions modernity's unrestrained quest for technological power. [Author] C. S. Lewis warned us of a society that has explained away every mystery, and the danger of what he calls "man-molders." He states that "the man-molders of the new age will be armed with the powers of an omni-competent state and an irresistible scientific technique: we shall get at last a race of conditioners who really can cut out all posterity in what shape they please." In his book *The Technological Society*, Jacques Ellul argues that we have come to the place where rationally arrived-at methods and absolute efficiency are all that really matters.

Let's consider the many voices warning us of the unintended consequences of modern technology.

Three Dangerous Technologies

Bill Joy argues that humanity is in danger from technologies that he believes are just around the corner. His concern is that robotics, genetic engineering, and nanotechnology present risks unlike anything we have created in the past. The key to understanding these new risks is the fact that these technologies share one remarkable potential; that is, self-replication. With all the present talk of weapons of mass destruction, Joy is more concerned about weapons of knowledge-enabled mass destruction. Joy writes:

> I think it is no exaggeration to say that we are on the cusp of the further perfection of extreme evil, an evil whose possibility spreads well beyond that which weapons of mass destruction bequeathed to the nation-states, on to a surprising and terrible empowerment of extreme individuals.

Joy believes that we will have intelligent robots by 2030, nano-replicators by 2020, and that the genetic revolution is already upon us. We all have a picture of what an intelligent robot might look like. Hollywood has given us many stories of that kind of technology gone wrong. . . .

The big debate today is whether or not true artificial intelligence is possible. Some like Danny Hillis, co-founder of Thinking Machines Corporation, believe that humans will probably merge with computers at some point. He says, "I'm as fond of my body as anyone, but if I can be 200 with a body of silicon, I'll take it." The human brain would provide the intelligence that computer science has yet to create for smart robots. The combination of human and silicon could make self-replicating robots a reality and challenge the existence of mankind, as we know it today.

Nanotechnology is used to construct very small machines. IBM recently announced that it has succeeded in creating a computer circuit composed of individual carbon monoxide atoms, a remarkable breakthrough. Although dreamed about since the 1950's, nanotechnology has recently made significant progress towards the construction of molecular-level "assemblers" that could solve a myriad of problems for humanity. They could construct low cost solar power materials, cures for diseases, inexpensive pocket supercomputers, and almost any product of which one could dream. However, they could also be made into weapons, self-replicating weapons. Some have called this the "gray goo" problem. For example, picture molecular sized machines that destroy all edible plant life over a large geographic area.

Surprisingly, Bill Joy concludes "The only realistic alternative I see is relinquishment: to limit development of the technologies that are too dangerous by limiting our pursuit of certain kinds of knowledge."

The End of Humanity?

History is filled with people who believed that they were racially superior to others; Nazi Germany is one obvious example. An aspect of America's uniqueness is the belief that all people are created equal and have rights endowed to them by their Creator that cannot easily be taken away. But what if it became overtly obvious that people are not equal, that some, because they could afford new genetic therapy, could have children that were brighter, stronger, and generally more capable than everyone else? This is the question being asked by Francis Fukuyama in his book *Our Posthuman Future*. The answer he comes up with is not comforting.

He contends that technology is at hand to separate humans into distinct genetic camps and that we will not hesitate to use it.

Fukuyama gives us three possible scenarios for the near future. First, he points to the rapid acceptance and widespread use of psychotropic drugs like Prozac and Ritalin as an indication that future mind altering drugs will find a receptive market. What if neuropharmacology continues to advance to the point where psychotropic drugs can be tailored to an individual's genetic makeup in order to make everyone "happy," without the side effects of the current drugs? It might even become possible to adopt different personalities on different days, extroverted and gregarious on Friday, reserved and contemplative for classes or work on Monday.

Which Planetary Civilization Shall the People of Earth Emulate?

It might be a familiar progression, transpiring on many worlds—a planet, newly formed, placidly revolves around its star; life slowly forms; a kaleidoscopic procession of creatures evolves; intelligence emerges which, at least up to a point, confers enormous survival value; and then technology is invented. It dawns on them that there are such things as laws of Nature, that these laws can be revealed by experiment, and that knowledge of these laws can be made both to save and to take lives, both on unprecedented scales. Science, they recognize, grants immense powers. In a flash, they create world-altering contrivances. Some planetary civilizations see their way through, place limits on what may and what must not be done, and safely pass through the time of perils. Others, not so lucky or so prudent, perish.

Carl Sagan, *Pale Blue Dot*, 1994.

Next, advances in stem cell research might soon allow us to regenerate any tissue in the body. The immediate result would be to dramatically extend normal human life expectancy, which could have a number of unpleasant social and economic implications. Finally, the feasibility of wealthy parents being able to screen embryos before they are placed in the womb is almost upon us. It would be hard to imagine parents denying their offspring the benefit of genetically enhanced intelligence, or the prospect of living longer lives free from genetic disease.

What will happen to civil rights within democratic nations if these predictions come true? Will we end up with a society split into subspecies with different native abilities and opportunities? What if Europe, for instance, is populated with relatively old, healthy, rich people and Africa continues to suffer economic deprivation with a far younger population ravaged by AIDS and other preventable diseases?

Interestingly, Fukuyama believes that the greatest reason not to employ some of these new technologies is that they would alter what it means to be human, and with that our notions of human dignity.

The Christian basis for human dignity is the *imago Dei*, the image of God placed within us by our Creator. Many are questioning the wisdom of chemical and genetic manipulation of humanity, even if it seems like a good idea now.

Early Warnings

There is a long Christian tradition of looking at the surrounding world with suspicion. Whether it's Tertullian asking the question "what has Athens to do with Jerusalem," or the Mennonite's promotion of simplicity and separation, Christians everywhere have had to struggle with the admonition to be in the world but not of it. Recent advances in science and technology are not making this struggle any easier.

In his work *The Abolition of Man*, C. S. Lewis argued that humanity's so-called power over nature "turns out to be a power exercised by some men over other men with Nature as its instrument." His concern is that the modern omnicompetent state combined with irresistible scientific techniques will result in Conditioners who have full control over the future of humankind. He feared that modernism and its ability to explain away everything but "nature" would leave us emptied of humanity. All that would be left is our animal instincts. The choice we have is to see humanity as a complex combination of both material and spiritual components or else to be reduced to machines made of meat ruled by other machines with nothing other than natural impulses to guide them.

Lewis writes:

> For the wise men of old the cardinal problem had been how to conform the soul to reality, and the solution had been knowledge, self-discipline, and virtue. For magic and applied science alike the problem is how to subdue reality to the wishes of men: the solution is a technique; and both, in the practice of this technique, are readying to do things hitherto regarded as disgusting and impious.

The issue of technique and its standardizing effects was

central to the thinking of sociologist Jacques Ellul in *The Technological Society*. Ellul argues that as a society becomes more technological it also becomes less interested in human beings. As he puts it, the technical world is the world of material things. When it does show an interest in mankind, it does so by converting him into a material object. Ellul warns that as technological capabilities grow, they result in greater and greater means to accomplish tasks than ever before, and he believes that the line between good and evil slowly disappears as this power grows.

Ellul worries that the more dependent we become on technology and technique, the more it conforms our behavior to its requirements rather than vice versa. Whether in corporate headquarters or on military bases much has been written about the de-humanizing effect of the employment of modern technique.

Primarily, he fears that even the church might become enamored with the results of technique. The result would be depending less on the power of God to work through Spirit-filled believers and more on our modern organization and technological skills.

A Principled Approach to Technology

Without a doubt, technology can help to make a society more productive, and growing productivity is a major predictor for future increases in standards of living. Likewise, technology results in greater opportunities to amass wealth both as a society and for individuals. Communication technology can help to unify a society as well as equalize access to information and thus promote social mobility.

On the other hand, technology can cause harm to both the environment and individuals. The Chernobyl nuclear power disaster in Russia and the Bhopal industrial gas tragedy in India resulted in thousands of deaths due to technological negligence. The widespread access to pornography over the Internet is damaging untold numbers of marriages and relationships. Terrorists have a growing number of inexpensive technologies available to use against civilians including anthrax and so-called radioactive dirty bombs that depend on recent technological advances.

However, it must be said that most Christians do not view technology itself as evil. Technology has remarkable potential for expanding the outreach of ministries and individuals. Probe's [a Christian organization] Web site is accessed by close to 100,000 people every month from over one hundred different countries. Modern communications technology makes it possible to broadcast the Gospel to virtually any place on the planet around the clock.

However, in our use of technology, Christians need to keep two principles in mind. First, we cannot give in to the modern tendency to define every problem and solution in scientific or technological terms. Since the Enlightenment, there has been a temptation to think naturalistically, reducing human nature and the rest of Creation to its materialistic component. The Bible speaks clearly of an unseen spiritual world and that we fight against these unseen forces when we work to build God's kingdom on earth. Ephesians tells us "our struggle is not against flesh and blood, but against the rulers, against the authorities, against the powers of this dark world and against the spiritual forces of evil in the heavenly realms." Scientific techniques alone will not further God's kingdom. We must acknowledge that prayer and the spiritual disciplines are necessary to counter the adversary.

Second, we need to remember the power that sin has to tempt us and to mar our thinking. The types of technologies and their uses should be limited and controlled by biblical ethics, not by our desires for more power or wealth. We are to have dominion over the earth as God's stewards, not as autonomous tyrants seeking greater pleasure and comfort.

| *"Applying a reasonable-person standard to genetic enhancements should allay the more lurid fears of biotech opponents."*

Human Genetic Enhancement Will Benefit Humanity

Ronald Bailey

Parents should be allowed to make reasonable genetic enhancements in their children, claims Ronald Bailey in the following viewpoint. Such enhancements will allow people to live longer, healthier, and more successful lives, he contends. Once the safety of genetic engineering is established, applying the reasonable-person standard—asking whether a reasonable person would consent to the genetic enhancement—will prevent parental abuse of the technology, he asserts. Bailey is the science correspondent for *Reason*, a libertarian magazine.

As you read, consider the following questions:
1. According to Bailey, on what point do biotech opponents and champions agree?
2. What must be done with genetic enhancement technologies before they can be used to help people, in the author's view?
3. In the author's opinion, why is it doubtful that many parents will make trivial genetic enhancement choices?

What genetic enhancements should parents be allowed to make in their offspring when those biotech innovations become available and relatively safe? You might think it's far too early to worry about such questions. However, opponents of new biotech research such as Francis Fukuyama disagree.

"We may be about to enter into a posthuman future, in which technology will give us the capacity gradually to alter [human] essence over time," worries Fukuyama in his new book *Our Posthuman Future*. Champions of the biotech future are with Fukuyama on this point: "We are on the cusp of profound biological change, poised to transcend our current form and character on a journey to destinations of new imagination," declares Gregory Stock in his new book, *Redesigning Humans*.

Let's assume that cheap, reliable genetic interventions will be available to parents in the next couple of decades. One such technology might involve inserting artificial chromosomes carrying genes selected by parents into an embryo at the one-cell stage. Once the artificial chromosomes have been incorporated into the embryo's genome, the selected genes would spread normally so that they would be in every cell of the enhanced child's body when he or she is born. Assuming something like artificial chromosomes will work, what limits, if any, should be put on parents' choices?

Answering the Critics

Opponents object that genetic enhancement technologies will not be safe, at least initially. Of course any enhancement technologies will have to be thoroughly tested in animals before they can be used to help people. Fortunately, our quickly advancing understanding of the complex web of interactions between genes and other cellular activities is likely to dramatically reduce the risks that might accompany inserting beneficial genes. As a general rule, no attempts at genetic enhancement should be attempted until solid research indicates that the risk of birth defects using genetic enhancement technologies is at least no greater than the risks of birth defects in children who are produced in the conventional way.

Skeptics about biotech also protest that genetically enhancing embryos will necessarily have to be done without their permission, thus violating moral prohibitions against

The ABCs of Human Genetic Engineering

If scientists were to begin altering the human genome, a woman's egg would first be removed from her body and fertilized through in vitro fertilization, creating an embryo. The embryo is copied through cloning, and new genes are spliced into each embryo's germline—the genetic blueprint created from the genetic material contained in sperm and egg cells. Each cell in an organism resulting from the embryo will contain the new gene. Any physiological changes caused by the new gene, such as resistance to cancer or increased memory, could be passed on to future generations through normal reproduction.

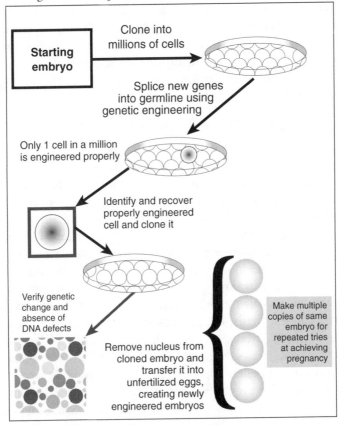

David Masci, *CQ Researcher*, 2001.

experimenting on human beings without their consent. Keep in mind that none of us gave our consent to be born, much less to be born with the specific complement of genes that we bear. Nevertheless, there is a way to address the opponents' concern over consenting to genetic enhancement: Would a reasonable person consent to having particular genetic traits or not?

Applying this standard would rule out allowing parents to select genes that would unquestionably harm their children. For example, no reasonable person would want to suffer from sickle-cell anemia or cystic fibrosis. This standard would also rule out the . . . reported quest by two deaf partners to have a congenitally deaf child. When that deaf couple approached a sperm bank seeking sperm from a deaf donor, the sperm bank rightly turned them away, explaining that congenital deafness is exactly the type of condition that rules out would-be donors. It is simply immoral to decide in advance to limit a child's potential. We already forbid such activities; we call them child abuse and punish those who harm children (or anybody else) on purpose.

A Reasonable-Person Standard

So what type of genetic enhancements would be morally acceptable? Again, applying a reasonable-person standard, consent can be presumed for general capacities that anyone would want, e.g., genes that tend to increase intelligence, strengthen immune systems, and lengthen lives. After all, these are capacities that many other people already have naturally, so it's hard to see a moral reason for denying them to others who will be able to obtain them safely by means of genetic engineering.

Opponents of genetic enhancement try to frighten the public by trivializing the choices that parents might make. They suggest that some parents will want to genetically engineer piano prodigies or professional basketball players. Others insinuate Nazi eugenics by hinting that some parents will choose to endow their children with blond hair and blue eyes. Some have even suggested that black parents might choose to genetically engineer their children so that they will have white skin in order for them to avoid the pain of racism.

It is doubtful that many parents will make such trivial

choices if implementing them would pose even the slightest risk to the health of their children. Choosing to engineer in genes that improve a child's health may be worth some small risk, but trying to insert genes for red hair would likely not be. However, in order to avoid rare cases of parental misconduct, it may be necessary to limit by law the choice of genetic interventions to the types of general capacities described above.

What about the far future? Someday might not parents choose to give their children gills or wings or some such other outlandish genetic combination? Even if such scenarios would be possible, they are unlikely. After all, human beings didn't sprout wings in order to fly, nor grow gills in order to swim underwater. Instead of modifying our genes, humanity will develop new technologies that will enable us to go where we want to go and do what we want to do.

Finally, applying a reasonable-person standard to genetic enhancements should allay the more lurid fears of biotech opponents and help citizens and policy makers as they craft institutions to guide the safe development of human genetic engineering.

"We don't need to go post-human, . . . to change ourselves in the thoroughgoing ways that the apostles of these new technologies demand."

Human Genetic Enhancement Is Unnecessary

Bill McKibben

Although human beings are not perfect, they are good enough and do not need genetic enhancement, maintains Bill McKibben in the following viewpoint. Human imperfection is what makes us human, argues McKibben. Moreover, using genetic enhancement to make us smarter, more attractive, or immortal appeals to humanity's superficial desires, he claims. Genetically enhancing children will leave humans as semi-robots, McKibben asserts. McKibben, an environmentalist, is author of *Enough: Staying Human in an Engineered Age.*

As you read, consider the following questions:

1. What dilemmas did cracking the atom raise that might also apply to cracking the gene, in McKibben's view?
2. According to the author, with what will those who support genetic enhancements replace fate and free will?
3. In the author's opinion, why is the human mind the apex of thinking machinery?

The 50th anniversary of the [discovery of the] double helix [structure of DNA] has been greeted with worldwide hoopla. It began in February [2003], the month that James Watson and Francis Crick actually made their discovery, and will culminate [in April 2003] with the golden anniversary of the paper they published announcing the news to the world.

The celebration is appropriate; understanding of the gene is rivaled only by understanding of the atom as the great scientific achievement of the last century. But just as cracking the atom raised the deepest ethical and practical dilemmas, so too does cracking the gene. Our new knowledge of genetic manipulation forces us to ask a question other generations couldn't have imagined: Are we a good enough species?

Manipulating Offspring

Consider Watson, who has been the towering figure in genetics research since that first paper—the "commanding general" of the DNA revolution, in the words of London's *Guardian*. He has used his fame and influence to push for changing human beings in the most radical ways. Human embryos should be manipulated, he has said, to increase intelligence, to eliminate shyness, even to make sure there are no "ugly babies."

In a documentary aired in Britain in March [2003], he called for using genetic tinkering to guard against the birth of the "really stupid." Others, citing successful animal tests on changing sociability patterns, have suggested we will soon be manipulating our offspring to be more optimistic or artistic or even devout.

Attempts to alter the human body are nothing new, of course. A century ago, French physiologist Charles Edouard Brown-Sequard became "the father of steroids" when he injected himself with an extract derived from the testicles of a guinea pig and a dog. But the latest plans of Watson and his followers are monstrous in an entirely new way. They look forward to a world of catalog children, who might spend their entire lives wondering which of their impulses are real and which the product of embryonic intervention. They replace the fate and the free will that always have been at the center of human meaning with a kind of genetic predestination that will leave our children as semi-robots.

More, though, they posit humans as in need of radical overhaul and design. Our minds aren't fast enough, the techno-zealots insist. We could have bigger muscles, perpetual Prozac.

Making Humans into Objects

Germ line manipulation opens up, for the first time in human history, the possibility of consciously designing human beings, in a myriad of different ways. I am not generally happy about using the concept of playing God, but it is difficult to avoid in this case. The advocates of genetic engineering point out that humans constantly 'play God', in a sense, by interfering with nature. Yet the environmental crisis has forced us to realise that many of the ways we already do this are not wise, destroy the environment and cannot be sustained. Furthermore, HGE [human genetic engineering] is not just a continuation of existing trends. Once we begin to consciously design ourselves, we will have entered a completely new era of human history, in which human subjects, rather than being accepted as they are will become just another kind of object, shaped according to parental whims and market forces.

David King, Human Genetics Alert, www.hgalert.org, n.d.

Most of all, say some, we might be able to dramatically postpone our demise. Scientists tinkering with the genes of other species have tripled their life spans. Michael D. West, chief executive of the prominent genetics firm Advanced Cell Technology, has confessed that his work is driven by fears of dying.

"All I think about, all day long, every day, is human mortality and our own aging," he said.

Finding Meaning in Human Limitations

Hopes of enhancement and immortality are widely and superficially appealing, drawing on the overpowering love we feel for our children and on our weakness for technological consumerism. It's all too easy to imagine that a society that celebrates botulism toxin injections to fight wrinkles might fall for gene injections that seemed to promise a ticket to Harvard, not to mention immortality. But they reflect the shallowest idea about human life—the sense that more is always better. In fact, it is in our limitations that we find our meaning. An eternal robot might be nifty, but it wouldn't be human.

Gregory Stock, director of the program in medicine, technology and society at UCLA [University of California at Los Angeles], has written that "the human mind cannot be the highest summit of cognitive performance." Measured in computations per second, that's certainly true; heck, an executive at Advanced Cell Technology has predicted that scientists soon will be able to add 20 or 30 IQ points to an embryo. But the human mind may nonetheless be the apex of thinking machinery simply because it is able to hold things in balance, to understand that more can be too much and that there are thresholds we don't need to cross.

What we need are the equivalents of Albert Einstein and Robert Oppenheimer, scientists who recognized that the swords they'd fashioned were sharpened keenly on both edges and who worked to diminish the dangers.

If we are to stay on the human side of the future, we also need a new understanding, one at least as revolutionary as the double helix: the understanding that as a species we are good enough. Not perfect, but not in need of drastic redesign. We need to accept certain imperfections in ourselves in return for certain satisfactions.

Across the sweep of history, we've managed to make our societies gradually but steadily more humane, more caring. As individuals, at least in the Western world, we've managed to build long lives of general ease and comfort. We don't need to go post-human, to fast-forward our evolution, to change ourselves in the thoroughgoing ways that the apostles of these new technologies demand. We need not ban stem-cell research, but we should regulate it so that it doesn't raise the possibility of designer babies.

A species smart enough to discover the double helix should be wise enough to leave it more or less alone.

*"The next major energy crisis . . . should
have a severe impact, be global in scope,
and be difficult to solve."*

An Energy Crisis Will Harm Humanity's Future

Charles T. Maxwell

In the next twenty-five years, global oil production will no longer meet increases in demand, resulting in a global energy crisis, claims Charles T. Maxwell in the following viewpoint. Recommendations that nations simply increase oil production or turn to natural gas and coal will not prevent the crisis, he asserts. Oil and natural gas production have peaked, and burning coal creates pollution. Since producing more oil is unlikely, people will have to learn to conserve energy and pursue alternative energy sources to prevent conflicts between and within nations. Maxwell is a senior energy analyst at Weeden & Co., an institutional investment firm.

As you read, consider the following questions:

1. According to Maxwell, on what will people likely waste a good deal of time during the early years of the energy crisis?
2. What creative possibilities would an increase in the price of oil unleash, in the author's view?
3. In the author's opinion, why is increasing oil production beyond conventional estimates not a feasible solution?

The energy crisis we are in . . . is entirely different from the temporary problems we experienced in 1973–74, 1979–86, 1990–91 and 2000. Then, there were political issues: Some nations were willing and able to produce oil for our use and some were not. There was always sufficient worldwide geological capacity to produce additional barrels of crude oil to meet the world's needs.

No longer. In the next major energy crisis, that capacity will likely be eroded. So the crisis should have a severe impact, be global in scope, and be difficult to solve. Plainly, it will be unprecedented. What may emerge could well be a restructured world, as well as a restructured oil industry.

Three Waves

Over the next 25 years, a new world energy economy will arrive in three waves. We are near the top of the first and smallest one, a warning wave. A second more powerful wave likely will hit in the 2009–2010 period when the non-OPEC [Organization of Petroleum Exporting Countries] world may reach its all-time highest output of crude oil, subsequently declining to become ever more dependent on OPEC for incremental barrels of production. The final wave should break around 2020, or earlier, as even OPEC's vast reserves are tapped at a maximum rate of production. After that, oil volume should head down and keep falling, never to revive.

Then the world's energy companies and governments finally may begin to address new sources of energy to replace oil, and this issue should become the principal economic and political preoccupation for the rest of the century.

An international economic disturbance of this magnitude will create potential conflicts between nations and civil competition within societies. These could be a trial for us and for our children, made worse in the early years by our lack of preparation and our failure to understand what is already happening to us. There could be a good deal of time wasted in recrimination while we seek to pin responsibility on culprits and conspirators and demons: The oil companies, government regulators, Wall Street, the automobile companies, OPEC, the Arabs, gas-guzzling U.S. consumers and so on.

Eventually, we will have to get down to addressing the real issues. They are geological—the limits on supply—and they are human—the tendencies toward greater consumption.

A Production Problem

There will be many who claim that the root of the problem is that we are "running out of oil." This is not an accurate way to describe the situation. We are running out of the ability to produce 2% more barrels each year to meet world demand that increases about 2% annually. The potential loss of the incremental barrels of output in the non-OPEC world as early as 2009–2010 would put the availability of additional barrels—and power over the price at which the world's consumers might purchase them—in the hands of five OPEC nations: Saudi Arabia, Iraq, Kuwait, the United Arab Emirates and Iran. (Under some circumstances, Venezuela might be an additional member of the club.)

Depending on their perception of their own political and economic strength, these countries might decide to lift crude prices much faster than the rate of dollar inflation, thus initiating economic and social changes in energy use on a global basis.

For the period 1987 to 2003, the historical range of oil prices was approximately $10 to $40 per barrel, with an average of $20. For 2004 to 2010, the price range could be $30 to $60, with an average of $40. For 2011 to 2020, the range could be $50 to $100, with an average price of $70 per barrel.

Such prices would unleash both destruction and creativity throughout industry and finance. As occurred in the 1970s, the design of cars, trucks, ships, planes and trains would change, commercial buildings and homes would be modified; chemical and industrial processing and most machinery would be redesigned to emphasize fuel economy or substitute fuels; tax systems would be thoroughly overhauled, with changed incentives and penalties. Urban planning and residential patterns would change. Living standards might slip a bit and they would recover in different shape: Cooler rooms in winter and warmer rooms in summer, changing clothes instead of thermostats, taking quicker showers and buying fewer hot tubs, using less lighting, indoors and out, accepting smaller and lighter cars, walking and bicycling more, and using public transportation; these are the obvious changes to come. Europeans, who long ago forced themselves to accept this lifestyle by imposing high energy taxes, might at last receive an economic return on their investment, while the U.S. struggles to change.

Could all this really result from the lack of a few extra barrels of oil in the non-OPEC world, and only five or six years out? Actually, a crisis could develop even earlier if one or two of the main OPEC producers were closed down for an extended period by a political or military emergency.

Close to 40% of global energy consumption is based on petroleum. Currently, we are utilizing about 98% of our world crude oil-producing capacity. The system should be considered stressed at a 95% utilization rate. We are no longer investing enough to lift capacity additions above the level of future demand growth on a consistent basis.

Alternatives to Oil

Greater use of natural gas would help, if adequate supplies were available at reasonable cost. However, in North America, the problems of obtaining gas are similar to those of obtaining oil. The U.S.'s natural-gas output appears already to have peaked. Canada can produce a bit more, but not enough to meet its own needs, along with ours, for the next decade. Europe might have an easier situation switching some oil demand over to gas, but new gas supplies would have to be transported long distances by pipeline from Russia, Turkmenistan, Iran, Algeria, and four or five countries of the Arab Middle East or by liquid-natural-gas tanker from Nigeria, Trinidad, or the Gulf. These incremental gas volumes would not come cheaply, quickly or without political risk. Some major gas-production developments are starting up in China and Southeast Asia, but the infrastructure to transport this gas and distribute it to local markets is not yet ready for use, and may require many years before it is. Most critically, gas cannot easily or cheaply take over the role of oil as the major transportation fuel. So, in the next decade, natural gas can only stand in for some oil consumption.

Our ability to substitute more coal for oil is also circum-

Thompson. © 2000 by *Detroit Free Press*. Reproduced by permission.

scribed since the technology to burn coal cleanly is still under development, and our vast coal supplies cannot yet be utilized without changing public opinion on the environmental consequences or changing the technology to avoid pollutants. That goes double for nuclear power. Using a lot more of these two fuels in the near term cannot be done in any case, since it would take many years to bring new plants and equipment on line.

Understanding Oil Production

If substitution is not immediately available, what about increasing production beyond conventional estimates? Surely, if prices rose a bit, a substantial new supply could be made available to the market? In many commodities, this would be correct. But, not in crude oil. The great Shell Oil geophysicist, M. King Hubbert (1903–1989), outlined the reasons for this in the mid-1950s when he predicted that the peak of U.S. oil production would occur in the early 1970s (and, despite considerable skepticism about his prediction, he was right on target). His case was that oil explorers, entering a new geological basin searching for petroleum, would always choose the largest and most accessible fields to drill first, because that would maximize their early returns. This selection would delay until later the harder work, at higher unit costs, of finding midsize and smaller fields in the mature years of basin production.

In addition, he observed, as oil reservoirs approached the halfway point of the production levels they were eventually going to yield, daily output would peak and subsequently start down.

Hubbert's two principles do work in practical terms in oil fields. The depletion of recoverable reserves in oil fields whose production levels have gone beyond their halfway point is causing a decline today in the output in certain mature oil-producing areas of the U.S., Canada, the North Sea, Russia, China, Saudi Arabia, Iran, Venezuela and Indonesia, among the major producers. Each year now, some 4% to 5% of world crude production is depleted, and an equivalent amount must be found, developed and brought onstream to maintain the original production volume. A further 2% must be found, developed and made available to the market to cover global growth needs.

Few people outside the oil industry understand that 6% to 7% more oil must be found and made available to the market each year in order to meet 2% growth in world consumption. It's a huge job; and it is getting harder to do, as the potential reserve size of prospects we are drilling today is smaller, and the large, prolific fields found in the past are advancing along their decline curves. Currently, some 70% of the oil that is consumed comes from fields discovered 25 or more years ago. Most of the likely oil-bearing basins of the world have now been prospected, and the odds of vast new reserves suddenly making an appearance are low. Of course, relatively large individual discoveries will occasionally turn up in the years ahead, but not in size and number to suggest these finds can equal the substantially greater amount of supplies that are being burned up. . . . The world is consuming some 30 billion barrels a year, and we are finding less than one-third that amount. This is a far cry from the mid-1960s, when the world discovery rate peaked at an annual figure of over 45 billion barrels, and we were using something less than 15 billion barrels each year.

Perhaps new technology can produce more? New equipment and methods do allow us to produce more from present fields, and to exploit some smaller fields at lower cost. However, the last decade brought the greatest application of oil-field technology ever seen, and the angle of the downtrend in the number of barrels discovered each year has hardly changed. Furthermore, no devices are known to be under development now in the oil industry's labs that would dramatically change the basic trend. Technology doesn't seem to be moving fast enough to save us.

Three Choices

Our country's leaders have three main choices: Taking over someone else's oil fields; carrying on until the lights go out and Americans are freezing in the dark; or changing our life style by deep conservation while heavily investing in alternative energy sources at higher costs.

The first two choices can be only temporary palliatives. Taking over foreign energy fields would be against this country's principles, and, like most violations of principle, it wouldn't work. This strategy wouldn't protect us from war, terrorism and the exhaustion of our military and moral resources. Carrying on as we are until we crash looks more like "surrender" than "adjustment."

By elimination, if not by wisdom, we will eventually turn to a massive national and international conservation effort. It should be launched with further development of coal and nuclear energy, along with imported liquid natural gas, tight-sands gas, coal-bed methane, gas-to-liquids conversion, tar sands and wind power. (Solar and biomass are not yet sufficiently developed to play a leading role.)

Whenever we decide to confront this reality, the resulting program surely will require many years of investing vast amounts of capital. It could, therefore, pre-empt some other lines of investment in economies already strapped for adequate returns to support the promises they have made to their aging societies. Without discipline, mental and physical preparedness and an intelligent selection of priorities conceived early enough to keep us from wavering, we will not pass the oncoming test.

"New technologies increase the amount of recoverable oil, and market prices . . . encourage new exploration and development."

Humanity Will Develop New Energy Technologies and Tap New Sources

David Deming

Humanity will continue to develop more efficient technologies and discover new energy sources that will supply the world's future energy needs, argues David Deming in the following viewpoint. Despite dire predictions that the world will run out of oil, Deming claims, exploration continues to uncover new supplies that improved technologies can extract more efficiently. Moreover, he asserts, new extraction technology will reduce the high cost of unconventional oil sources such as rocks, shale, and tar sands. Deming is a geology and geophysics professor at the University of Oklahoma and a scholar with the National Center for Policy Analysis.

As you read, consider the following questions:

1. In Deming's view, what followed the "energy gap" predictions of the 1970s?
2. According to the author, what is the distinction between reserves and resources?
3. In the author's opinion, what is the primary problem with a Hubbert-style analysis?

O il is a nonrenewable resource. Every gallon of petroleum burned today is unavailable for use by future generations. Over the past 150 years, geologists and other scientists often have predicted that our oil reserves would run dry within a few years. When oil prices rise for an extended period, the news media fill with dire warnings that a crisis is upon us. Environmentalists argue that governments must develop new energy technologies that do not rely on fossil fuels. The facts contradict these harbingers of doom:

- World oil production continued to increase through the end of the 20th century.
- Prices of gasoline and other petroleum products, adjusted for inflation, are lower than they have been for most of the last 150 years.
- Estimates of the world's total endowment of oil have increased faster than oil has been taken from the ground.

How is this possible? We have not run out of oil because new technologies increase the amount of recoverable oil, and market prices—which signal scarcity—encourage new exploration and development. Rather than ending, the Oil Age has barely begun.

The History of Oil Prognostications

The history of the petroleum industry is punctuated by periodic claims that the supply will be exhausted, followed by the discovery of new oil fields and the development of technologies for recovering additional supplies. For instance:

- Before the first U.S. oil well was drilled in Pennsylvania in 1859, petroleum supplies were limited to crude oil that oozed to the surface. In 1855, an advertisement for Kier's Rock Oil advised consumers to "hurry, before this wonderful product is depleted from Nature's laboratory."
- In 1874, the state geologist of Pennsylvania, the nation's leading oil-producing state, estimated that only enough U.S. oil remained to keep the nation's kerosene lamps burning for four years.

Seven such oil shortage scares occurred before 1950. As a writer in the *Oil Trade Journal* noted in 1918:

At regularly recurring intervals in the quarter of a century that I have been following the ins and outs of the oil business, there has always arisen the bugaboo of an approaching oil famine, with plenty of individuals ready to prove that the commercial supply of crude oil would become exhausted within a given time—usually only a few years distant.

1973 Oil Embargo. The 1973 Arab oil embargo gave rise to renewed claims that the world's oil supply would be exhausted shortly. "The Oil Crisis: This Time the Wolf Is Here," warned an article in the influential journal *Foreign Affairs.* Geologists had cried wolf many times, acknowledged the authors of a respected and widely used textbook on economic geology in 1981; "finally, however, the wolves are with us." The authors predicted that the United States was entering an incipient 125-year-long "energy gap," projected to be at its worst shortly after the year 2000.

The predictions of the 1970s were followed in a few years by a glut of cheap oil:

- The long-term inflation-adjusted price of oil from 1880 through 1970 averaged $10 to $20 a barrel.
- The price of oil soared to over $50 a barrel in inflation-adjusted 1996 U.S. dollars following the 1979 political revolution in Iran.
- But by 1986, inflation-adjusted oil prices had collapsed to one-third their 1980 peak.

When projected crises failed to occur, doomsayers moved their predictions forward by a few years and published again in more visible and prestigious journals:

- In 1989, one expert forecast that world oil production would peak that very year and oil prices would reach $50 a barrel by 1994.
- In 1995, a respected geologist predicted in *World Oil* that petroleum production would peak in 1996, and after 1999 major increases in crude oil prices would have dire consequences. He warned that "[m]any of the world's developed societies may look more like today's Russia than the U.S."
- A 1998 *Scientific American* article entitled "The End of Cheap Oil" predicted that world oil production would peak in 2002 and warned that "what our society does face, and soon, is the end of the abundant and cheap oil on which all industrial nations depend."

Similar admonitions were published in the two most influential scientific journals in the world, *Nature* and *Science*. A 1998 article in *Science* was titled "The Next Oil Crisis Looms Large—and Perhaps Close." A 1999 *Nature* article was subtitled "[A] permanent decline in global oil production rate is virtually certain to begin within 20 years."

A New Source of Energy Will Come

Whatever ends up replacing petroleum will come in its own good time, later than we'd like but probably sooner than we expect. It will come because it stores energy and power better than gasoline does and more cheaply to boot. It will come with some tremendous benefits and some unfortunate drawbacks. Consider as you lament the evils of crude oil: the fairly accidental discovery of kerosene and expansion of the refining process in the second half of the 19th century saved whales from an early mass extinction while at the same time making nighttime light and winter heat affordable to even the most impoverished parts of Asia, Africa and Latin America. Gasoline itself was originally a waste product, largely unused until the invention of the internal combustion engine, and automobiles made for cleaner streets (no more manure) and safer farm equipment, given that farmers no longer had to wrestle with motors that had minds of their own.

Charles Featherstone, "The Myth of 'Peak Oil,'" www.mises.org, January 12, 2005.

1990s Oil Glut. However, rather than falling, world oil production continued to increase throughout the 1990s. Prices have not skyrocketed, suggesting that oil is not becoming more scarce:

- Oil prices were generally stable at $20 to $30 a barrel throughout the 1990s.
- In 2001, oil prices fell to a 30-year low after adjusting for inflation.
- Furthermore, the inflation-adjusted retail price of gasoline, one of the most important derivatives of oil, fell to historic lows in the past few years.

Reserves Versus Resources

Nonexperts, including some in the media, persistently predict oil shortage because they misunderstand petroleum terminology. Oil geologists speak of both reserves and resources.

- *Reserves* are the portion of *identified* resources that can be economically extracted and exploited using current technology.
- *Resources* include all fuels, both identified and unknown, and constitute the world's endowment of fossil fuels.

Oil reserves are analogous to food stocks in a pantry. If a household divides its pantry stores by the daily food consumption rate, the same conclusion is always reached: the family will starve to death in a few weeks. Famine never occurs because the family periodically restocks the pantry.

Similarly, if oil reserves are divided by current production rates, exhaustion appears imminent. However, petroleum reserves are continually increased by ongoing exploration and development of resources. For 80 years, oil reserves in the United States have been equal to a 10- to 14-year supply at current rates of development. If they had not been continually replenished, we would have run out of oil by 1930.

How Much Oil Is Left?

Scaremongers are fond of reminding us that the total amount of oil in the Earth is finite and cannot be replaced during the span of human life. This is true; yet estimates of the world's total oil endowment have grown faster than humanity can pump petroleum out of the ground.

The Growing Endowment of Oil. Estimates of the total amount of oil resources in the world grew throughout the 20th century.

- In May 1920, the U.S. Geological Survey announced that the world's total endowment of oil amounted to 60 billion barrels.
- In 1950, geologists estimated the world's total oil endowment at around 600 billion barrels.
- From 1970 through 1990, their estimates increased to between 1,500 and 2,000 billion barrels.
- In 1994, the U.S. Geological Survey raised the estimate to 2,400 billion barrels, and their most recent estimate (2000) was of a 3,000-billion-barrel endowment.

By the year 2000, a total of 900 billion barrels of oil had been produced. Total world oil production in 2000 was 25 billion barrels. If world oil consumption continues to increase at an average rate of 1.4 percent a year, and no further resources are discovered, the world's oil supply will not be exhausted until the year 2056.

Additional Petroleum Resources. The estimates above do not include unconventional oil resources. *Conventional* oil refers to oil that is pumped out of the ground with minimal processing; *unconventional* oil resources consist largely of tar sands and oil shales that require processing to extract liquid petroleum. Unconventional oil resources are very large. In the future, new technologies that allow extraction of these unconventional resources likely will increase the world's reserves.

- Oil production from tar sands in Canada and South America would add about 600 billion barrels to the world's supply.
- Rocks found in the three western states of Colorado, Utah and Wyoming alone contain 1,500 billion barrels of oil.
- Worldwide, the oil-shale resource base could easily be as large as 14,000 billion barrels—more than 500 years of oil supply at year 2000 production rates.

Unconventional oil resources are more expensive to extract and produce, but we can expect production costs to drop with time as improved technologies increase efficiency.

The Role of Technology

With every passing year it becomes possible to exploit oil resources that could not have been recovered with old technologies. The first American oil well drilled in 1859 by Colonel Edwin Drake in Titusville, Pa.—which was actually drilled by a local blacksmith known as Uncle Billy Smith—reached a total depth of 69 feet (21 meters).

- Today's drilling technology allows the completion of wells up to 30,000 feet (9,144 meters) deep.
- The vast petroleum resources of the world's submerged continental margins are accessible from offshore platforms that allow drilling in water depths to 9,000 feet (2,743 meters).
- The amount of oil recoverable from a single well has greatly increased because new technologies allow the

boring of multiple horizontal shafts from a single vertical shaft.

- Four-dimensional seismic imaging enables engineers and geologists to see a subsurface petroleum reservoir drain over months to years, allowing them to increase the efficiency of its recovery.

New techniques and new technology have increased the efficiency of oil exploration. The success rate for exploratory petroleum wells has increased 50 percent over the past decade, according to energy economist Michael C. Lynch.

Examining Predictions of Declining Production

Despite these facts, some environmentalists claim that declining oil production is inevitable, based on the so-called Hubbert model of energy production. They ignore the inaccuracy of Hubbert's projections.

Problems with Hubbert's Model. In March 1956, M. King Hubbert, a research scientist for Shell Oil, predicted that oil production from the 48 contiguous United States would peak between 1965 and 1970. Hubbert's prediction was initially called "utterly ridiculous." But when U.S. oil production peaked in 1970, he became an instant celebrity and living legend.

Hubbert based his estimate on a mathematical model that assumes the production of a resource follows a bell-shaped curve—one that rises rapidly to a peak and declines just as quickly. In the case of petroleum, the model requires an accurate estimate of the size of the total oil endowment. His best estimate of the size of petroleum resources in the lower 48 states was 150 billion barrels. His high estimate, which he considered an exaggeration, was 200 billion barrels.

Based on these numbers, Hubbert produced two curves showing a "best" estimate of U.S. oil production and a "high" estimate. The claimed accuracy of Hubbert's predictions are largely based on the upper curve—his absolute upper limit.

- Hubbert set the absolute upper limit for peak U.S. oil production at roughly 3 billion barrels a year, and his best or lower estimate of peak future U.S. crude oil production was closer to 2.5 billion barrels.

- As early as 1970, actual U.S. crude oil production exceeded Hubbert's upper limit by 13 percent.
- By the year 2000, actual U.S. oil production from the lower 48 states was 2.5 times higher than Hubbert's 1956 "best" prediction.

Production in the 48 contiguous states peaked, but at much higher levels than Hubbert predicted. From about 1975 through 1995, Hubbert's upper curve was a fairly good match to actual U.S. production data. But in recent years, U.S. crude oil production has been consistently higher than Hubbert considered possible.

Hubbert's 1980 prediction of U.S. oil production, his last, was substantially less accurate than his 1956 "high" estimate. In the year 2000, actual U.S. oil production from the lower 48 states was 1.7 times higher than his 1980 revised prediction.

In light of this, it is strange that Hubbert's predictions have been characterized as remarkably successful. While production in the United States is declining, as Hubbert predicted, it is doing so at a much slower rate. Furthermore, lower production does not necessarily indicate the looming exhaustion of U.S. oil resources. It shows instead that at current prices and with current technology, less of the remaining petroleum is economically recoverable.

Hubbert's Prediction for Natural Gas. In 1998, Peter McCabe of the U.S. Geological Survey showed that energy resources do not necessarily follow Hubbert-type curves, and even if they do a decline in production may not be due to exhaustion of the resource.

For example, Hubbert also predicted future U.S. natural gas production. This prediction turned out to be grossly wrong. As of 2000, U.S. natural gas production was 2.4 times higher than Hubbert had predicted in 1956.

The Production Curve for Coal. Production of anthracite coal in Pennsylvania through the 19th and 20th centuries followed a Hubbert-type curve more closely than any other known energy resource. Production started around 1830, peaked around 1920, and by 1995 had fallen to about 5 percent of its peak value. However, the supply of Pennsylvania anthracite coal is far from exhausted. If production were to resume at the all-time high rate of 100 million short tons per year, the resource base would support 190 years of production. Production declined not because the resource was depleted but because people stopped heating their homes with coal and switched to cleaner-burning oil and gas.

The primary problem with a Hubbert-type analysis is that it requires an accurate estimate of the total resource endowment. Yet estimates of the total endowment have grown systematically larger for at least 50 years as technology has made it possible to exploit petroleum resources previously not considered economical. Hubbert-type analyses of oil production have systematically underestimated future oil production. This will continue to be the case until geologists can produce an accurate and stable estimate of the size of the total oil endowment.

Is an Oil Economy Sustainable?

In the long run, an economy that utilizes petroleum as a primary energy source is not sustainable, because the amount of oil in the Earth's crust is finite. However, *sustainability* is a misleading concept, a chimera. No technology since the birth of civilization has been sustainable. All have been replaced as people devised better and more efficient technologies. The history of energy use is largely one of substitution. In the 19th century, the world's primary energy source was wood. Around 1890, wood was replaced by coal. Coal remained the world's largest source of energy until the 1960s when it was replaced by oil. We have only just entered the petroleum age.

How long will it last? No one can predict the future, but the world contains enough petroleum resources to last at least until the year 2100. This is so far in the future that it would be ludicrous for us to try to anticipate what energy sources our descendants will utilize. Over the next several decades the world likely will continue to see short-term spikes in the price of oil, but these will be caused by political instability and market interference—not by an irreversible decline in supply.

Periodical Bibliography

The following articles have been selected to supplement the diverse views presented in this chapter.

Mary H. Cooper	"Alternative Fuels," *CQ Researcher*, February 25, 2005.
Mary H. Cooper	"Energy Policy," *CQ Researcher*, May 25, 2001.
James Crabtree	"Internet Is Bad for Democracy," *Japan Today*, March 30, 2005.
Charles Featherstone	"The Myth of 'Peak Oil,'" Ludwig von Mises Institute, January 12, 2005. www.mises.org.
Steve Fuller	"When History Outsmarts Computers," *Futures*, September 2003.
Brian Halweil and Dick Bell	"Beyond Cloning: The Larger Agenda of Human Engineering," *World Watch*, July/August 2002.
David Holcberg	"The Morality of Genetic Engineering," Ayn Rand Institute, June 25, 2001. www.aynrand.org.
Steven Johnson	"Dreaming of Electric Sheep," *Nation*, September 3, 2001.
Bill Joy	"Why the Future Doesn't Need Us," *Wired*, April 2000.
Michael T. Klare	"Crude Awakening," *Nation*, November 8, 2004.
Chuck Klosterman	"The Awe-Inspiring Majesty of Science," *Esquire*, October 2004.
Gene J. Koprowski	"The Future of Human Knowledge: The Semantic Web," *Tech News World*, July 28, 2003.
Stephen Leahy	"Biotech Hope and Hype: The Genetics Revolution Has Failed to Deliver," *Maclean's*, September 30, 2002.
Yuval Levin	"Imagining the Future," *New Atlantis*, Winter 2004.
David Manasian	"Digital Dilemmas," *Economist*, January 23, 2003.
David Masci	"Designer Humans," *CQ Researcher*, May 18, 2001.
Bill McKibben	"Why Environmentalists Should Be Concerned," *World Watch*, July/August 2002.

New Atlantis	"The Nanotech Schism," Winter 2004.
James Pethokoukis	"Our Biotech Bodies, Ourselves," *U.S. News & World Report*, May 31, 2004.
Tom Price	"Cyberpolitics," *CQ Researcher*, September 17, 2004.
Glenn Harlan Reynolds	"Environmental Regulation of Nanotechnology: Some Preliminary Observations," *Environmental Law Reporter*, June 2001.
Paul Roberts	"Over a Barrel," *Mother Jones*, November/December 2004.
Mark Williams	"The End of Oil?" *Technology Review*, February 2005.
Adam Wolfson	"Does Genetic Engineering Endanger Human Freedom?" *American Enterprise*, October 2001.

CHAPTER 2

What Is the Future of World Health?

Chapter Preface

Humanity's future depends upon maintaining the health and well-being of the world's children and their mothers. "Mothers, the newborn and children represent the well-being of a society and its potential for the future. Their health needs cannot be left unmet without harming the whole of society," argues Lee Jong-wook, director general of the World Health Organization (WHO). Nevertheless, in its 2005 report, *Mothers and Children Matter—So Does Their Health*, WHO reports that each year 3.3 million babies or maybe even more—are stillborn, more than 4 million die within 28 days of coming into the world, and a further 6.6 million young children die before their fifth birthday. Maternal deaths also continue unabated—the annual total now stands at 529,000 often sudden, unpredicted deaths which occur during pregnancy itself (some 68,000 as a consequence of unsafe abortion), during childbirth, or after the baby has been born—leaving behind devastated families. While few dispute the importance of maternal and infant health to humanity's future, analysts disagree over how best to ensure it.

Some commentators attribute the high rates of maternal and infant mortality to the marginalized status of women in many nations. The plight of mothers and children, claims Doctor Halfdan Mahler, former director general of WHO, is "deeply rooted in the adverse social, cultural and economic environments of society, and especially the environment that societies create for women." Women's lack of decision-making power and their unequal access to resources lead to their and their children's ill health, these analysts contend. Mahler argues, "Millions of women and their families live in a social environment that works against seeking and enjoying good health. Women often have limited exposure to the education, information and new ideas that could spare them from repeated childbearing and save their lives during childbirth. They may have no say in decisions on whether to use contraception or where to give birth." The solution, commentators such as Mahler argue, is to secure for all women the right to make their own reproductive health decisions and to make contraception information and education readily available.

Other experts believe that economic development will reduce infant and maternal mortality. They point to statistics showing that as income rises, mortality decreases. Since economic development improves the lives of women and children, these experts argue, it should also reduce infant and maternal mortality. "Development . . . increases female education, it expands women's opportunities and promotes their status, [and] it changes the cost and benefits of children and the demand for them," writes political economist Sloj S. Litofe. He maintains that development "weakens the motivation to have big family size." In this way, Litofe reasons, "lower fertility is likely to raise average per child levels of household expenditure on health and education, and thereby, improve the level of child health and education."

Some experts disagree with this analysis. According to Carla AbouZahr of the Joint United Nations Programme on HIV/AIDS, "What is lacking is not the level of national wealth, but the level of commitment to do something." She maintains, for example, that "the proportion of births attended by skilled personnel is a key indicator for tracking progress in reducing maternal mortality." Promoting economic growth is a long process that requires a significant financial investment while providing a skilled health worker to assist every delivery "would cost only about $3 a person a year in low-income countries," she asserts. "Reducing maternal mortality is not necessarily dependent on economic development," AbouZahr argues; it is a lack of commitment to act on behalf of women that "robs the next generation of hope for a better future."

The solution to the problem of infant and maternal mortality remains controversial. The authors in the following chapter debate other issues concerning the future of world health.

"An accelerating movement of people and goods has also been accompanied by growing threats of disease."

Globalization Is a Threat to World Health

Dennis Pirages and Theresa DeGeest

The increased movement of people and goods across the globe has accelerated the spread of disease, argue political scientists Dennis Pirages and Theresa DeGeest, authors of *Ecological Security: An Evolutionary Perspective on Globalization*, from which the following viewpoint is excerpted. Not only have many new diseases emerged and quickly spread since 1973, diseases such as malaria, once thought to be under control, have returned to kill millions, the authors claim. To control future outbreaks, they maintain, world health policy makers must diligently monitor disease and implement rapid response plans.

As you read, consider the following questions:

1. According to Pirages and DeGeest, what disease arrived during the period of increasing Western European commerce in the middle of the fourteenth century?
2. How many previously unknown diseases do the authors claim have been identified since 1973?
3. What diseases do the authors assert exact the greatest number of casualties?

There is overwhelming historical evidence that contact between previously isolated populations and ecosystems—or their integration into larger units—has created major evolutionary discontinuities and often exacted a tragic disease toll.

Microbial Disasters in Antiquity

William H. McNeill has observed that the expanding Roman Empire was repeatedly afflicted by strange maladies originating in the provinces. There were reportedly at least 11 microbial disasters during Republican times.

A major epidemic struck the city of Rome in 65 C.E., but that paled in comparison with a widespread pandemic that began to sweep through the entire empire in 165 C.E.

Mortality in this latter plague was heavy: It is estimated that one-quarter to one-third of those coming down with the disease died.

In more recent history, contacts between expanding European populations and those in other parts of the world had similarly serious disease ramifications.

By the middle of the 14th century, many of the small kingdoms of Western Europe had begun to increase commerce, not only with each other, but with countries of the Orient—courtesy of expanding trade routes between Europe and China.

During this period of economic growth, urban expansion and increasing trade, messengers, merchants and mercenaries were moving more freely among societies.

This increasing contact facilitated the spread of diseases to biologically naïve populations, the most infamous of these diseases being *Yersinia pestis*—also known as the Black Death.

Traveling with merchant caravans along trade routes from Asia, the black rat (*Rattus rattus*) carried disease-bearing fleas to Europe.

The arrival of the bubonic plague in 1346 began a destructive pandemic, and successive waves of disease cut the region's populations by nearly 40%—the highest mortality being in urban areas.

Contacts between previously separated people also resulted in heavy casualties during the age of European exploration and colonization.

For example, the ships of Christopher Columbus, arriving in the Caribbean in 1492, were the first of a wave of vessels that brought Europeans—and the microbes that accompanied them—to the Western Hemisphere.

Some of these microorganisms were responsible for eventually wiping out a significant portion of the indigenous peoples.

The military history of the period is filled with tales of miraculous conquests of huge numbers of indigenous peoples by mere handfuls of European troops. But in reality, there were no bonafide miracles.

Most of the damage was inflicted by diseases—particularly smallpox—that for the most part were unwittingly launched by the European invaders.

These new diseases killed approximately two-thirds of the people who encountered them, leaving societies in disarray and unable to muster a decent defense of their territories.

In the words of McNeill, "From the Amerindian point of view, stunned acquiescence to Spanish superiority was the only possible response. Native authority structures crumbled: The old gods seemed to have abdicated. The situation was ripe for the mass conversions recorded so proudly by Christian missionaries."

In the more contemporary world, an accelerating movement of people and goods has also been accompanied by growing threats of disease.

An Unanticipated Global Assault

During World War I, influenza traveled from Kansas to Europe along with American troops—and eventually caused more casualties worldwide than did the military hostilities.

And influenza pandemics have regularly spread around the world, sickening hundreds of millions—and killing tens of thousands.

There is now considerable evidence that pathogenic microorganisms are poised to launch new assaults on a global scale.

Many diseases that were thought to have been beaten into

submission are making a comeback. And some novel pathogens—to which few people are now immune—are emerging as serious threats to security.

Spread from Hotel M

Reported as of March 28, 2003

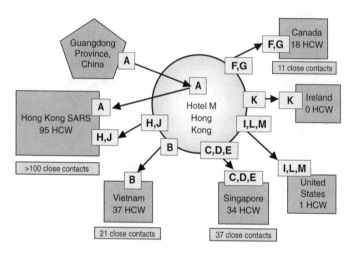

Known as "patient zero" (A in the chart above), professor Liu Jianlun, a renowned microbiologist who later died of SARS, arrived in Hong Kong on February 20, 2003, from Guangdong Province, Mainland China, and checked into the Metropole Hotel. The chart illustrates how quickly SARS spread. Liu was a *super spreader* who indirectly infected hundreds of people in 6 countries during his 24-hour stay in the hotel. HCW indicates a health care worker; individual patients are named with capital letters.

Ted Kaehler, www.cdc.gov, 2003.

Since 1973, 20 well-known diseases—including tuberculosis, malaria and cholera—have reemerged or spread geographically and at least 30 previously unknown diseases have been identified. Chief among these new diseases is the HIV/AIDS virus.

In an unprecedented move, HIV/AIDS was declared to be a threat to national security by the Clinton administration in April 2000.

And, of course, the new threat of biological warfare—and the possible introduction of genetically engineered pathogens—worsens the situation.

In spite of significant advances in medical technology, there are abundant indications that these new and resurgent diseases will be a continuing threat to ecological security.

Infectious diseases are already a leading cause of death, accounting for nearly 30% of the estimated annual fatalities around the world.

Continuing and Powerful Threats

Traditional diseases—such as respiratory infections, especially influenza and pneumonia, as well as diarrhea—currently exact the greatest number of casualties. But HIV/AIDS is rapidly growing in importance.

In 2000, 3.9 million people died from respiratory infections and 2.1 million people died from diarrheal diseases. At the same time, 2.9 million people died from AIDS. Some 42 million people are currently HIV positive. Five million people are newly infected with HIV each year.

Tuberculosis (TB) and malaria are the next most significant disease threats to human well-being. The World Health Organization declared TB to be a global emergency in 1993.

TB took the lives of 1.7 million people in 2000 and one-third of the world's population is infected with latent TB.

Drug resistance is a growing problem and nearly 50% of those with drug-resistant TB die despite treatment.

Malaria, a tropical disease that was thought to be under control in the 1970s and 1980s, is making a comeback. In 1998, 300 million people were estimated to be infected with malaria—and 1.1 million people died from the disease.

Most of the deaths occurred in countries of Sub-Saharan Africa, where increases of 7% to 20% annually are expected for the next several years.

Although they have not yet become major killers at this time—accounting for only about 600,000 deaths annually—hepatitis B and C pose a significant future threat.

Nearly 350 million people are chronic carriers of hepatitis B and some 170 million people are estimated to be infected with hepatitis C.

A State of Bioinsecurity

The nagging question is why—despite numerous technological breakthroughs and repeated claims that the threat of disease would soon be eradicated—does bioinsecurity remain so pervasive?

Both environmental degradation and changes in human behavior are making people more vulnerable to disease organisms.

There are at least seven kinds of environmental and behavioral changes that are now upsetting the human-microbe relationship.

They are:

1. Demographic dislocation
2. Technological innovation
3. Increased travel and commerce
4. Microbial adaptation
5. Behavioral changes
6. Persisting poverty
7. Environmental change

Building biosecurity requires moving beyond the wake-up call represented by HIV/AIDS and emerging bioterrorism —and addressing a series of long-term security issues raised by infectious diseases.

Existing institutions have been shaped and pruned by decades of complacency and budget-cutting in the mistaken belief that the battle against disease has been won.

The World Health Organization (WHO) was created in 1948 as the UN [United Nations] agency responsible for creating and disseminating international health regulations and guidelines, as well as to provide technical assistance to member countries.

But the WHO has been far from anticipatory or flexible in dealing with the changing disease challenges.

It wasn't until 1995 that a division was created to deal with emerging and contagious diseases. New leadership promises change, but member support will be essential to an effective response.

An effective biosecurity policy requires continuing surveillance and rapid response to disease outbreaks. Two surveillance networks have been established in order to monitor and assess disease outbreaks.

The WHO has set up a network called WHONET that links microbiology labs around the world to a central database devoted to detecting reservoirs of drug-resistant microbes and preventing their spread.

And a group of scientists in the United States has set up a Program to Monitor Emerging Diseases (ProMED), an electronic mail network that facilitates reporting on—and discussions of—disease outbreaks around the world.

While these are positive developments, it is of little use simply to report on disease outbreaks if no response capability exists.

The Centers for Disease Control and Prevention in the United States do send teams of epidemiologists to various countries where disease outbreaks occur. But the agency has had inadequate funding to broaden its role.

While the WHO would in theory be a logical choice to carry out the response function, it now lacks authority, funding, staff and facilities to do so.

Clearly much remains to be done in addressing diseases that can quickly move through all of the neighborhoods of the emerging global city.

"Globalisation, economic growth, and improvements in health go hand in hand."

Globalization Promotes World Health

Richard G.A. Feachem

Globalization promotes economic growth, which in turn improves world health, maintains Richard G.A. Feachem in the following viewpoint. While the health of people who live under isolationist governments is often poor, he argues, the health of those who reside in nations open to globalization is improving. Nations open to global trade enjoy increased income and greater access to health care services and technology, claims Feachem. Moreover, global Internet communication increases the spread of health care information, improves disease surveillance, and promotes the movement to protect women's rights, all of which improve world health. Feachem is director of the Institute for Global Health at the University of California, San Francisco.

As you read, consider the following questions:
1. In Feachem's opinion, what do antiglobalization protesters overlook?
2. With what does gross national product per capita correlate so strongly, in the author's view?
3. According to the author, why will the Internet have a substantial health impact in low- and middle-income countries?

Richard G.A. Feachem, "Globalisation Is Good for Your Health, Mostly," *British Medical Journal*, vol. 323, September 2001, pp. 504–506. Copyright © 2001 by the British Medical Association. Reproduced by permission.

We live in extraordinary times. Since [the anti-globalization protests of] December 1999 in Seattle, every meeting of the leaders of the World Trade Organisation, the World Bank, the International Monetary Fund, and the world's richest nations (the G8) has been met by increasingly large and violent demonstrations against global processes that are manifestly beneficial. The protestors comprise such a diverse array of groups and opinions that it is impossible to capture their message in a single phrase. . . . The central theme of the protests is discernible, however, and is something like: "Increasing global economic and social integration is a conspiracy by the rich and powerful to exploit the poor and underprivileged."

A Muddled Message

Beyond this central theme one hears strands that are against capitalism, economic growth, multinational companies, international institutions, and the governments of wealthy countries. Strangely, the protestors are muted or silent in their objection to the corrupt and inefficient governments of some low income countries or to the massive human rights abuses that occur daily in some poorer countries.

The protestors are right about two things. Firstly, poverty is indeed the most pressing moral, political, and economic issue of our time. Secondly, the tide of globalisation can be turned back. However, to reverse that tide would be, in the words of an *Economist* editorial, "an unparalleled catastrophe for the planet's most desperate people and something that could be achieved only by trampling down individual liberty on a daunting scale."

Many formal definitions of globalisation have been proposed. I think of it as openness: openness to trade, to ideas, to investment, to people, and to culture. It brings benefits today, as it has for centuries—and it also brings risks and adverse consequences, as it has for centuries.

There are three main flaws in the protesters' positions. Firstly, they overlook a substantial body of rigorous evidence on the economic benefits of globalisation. Secondly, they ignore the wider social and political benefits of globalisation. Thirdly, they lack a counter proposal—if not globalisation, then what?

The evidence that openness to trade and investment is good for economic growth is compelling and goes back several centuries. We can see this effect not only in the multi-country econometric analyses but also in the recent experiences of individual countries. China, India, Uganda, and Vietnam, for example, have all experienced surges in economic growth since liberalising their trade and inward investment policies. Because gross national product per capita correlates so strongly with national health status, we can conclude that, in general, openness to trade improves national health status.

Globalisation and Equity

However, evidence on associations between openness and growth among nations does not directly address issues of equity. . . . It has become common to assert that globalisation has increased inequity both among and within countries. Statements to this effect litter the literature on globalisation and health and are unquestioningly accepted as true in many public health forums. It is necessary to be critical and cautious about such statements. While it will always be possible to show some increasing wealth gaps—especially by comparing very poor countries with very rich countries or by comparing the poorest tenth with the richest tenth within a country—there is strong evidence in the counter direction. For example, globalising developing countries (those which increased trade and reduced import tariffs) have grown much faster than other developing countries. Importantly, they have also grown faster than the wealthy countries in the Organisation for Economic Cooperation and Development (OECD), therefore narrowing the wealth gap between rich and poor countries.

But what of intra-country equity? Again, . . . evidence is optimistic. Analysis of 137 countries shows that the incomes of the poorest 20% on average rise and fall in step with national growth or recession. In other words, on average, changes in national wealth are not systematically associated with income distribution. There is, however, considerable individual country variation around this average outcome, and studying the outliers in detail would be fruitful. Why is it that in some countries the poor benefit disproportionately from growth while in others they have been left behind. The answer surely lies in the detail of the economic and social policies in place in those countries at the time that national growth was occurring, and understanding these relationships in detail will help to ensure that the poor always benefit from growth.

A Global Health Revolution

At the time of the founding of the World Health Organization in 1948, the average global life expectancy was 46 years. Today, life expectancy has risen to 65 years. This huge increase has come in part from a global health revolution in which many U.S. institutions of higher learning have played an important role. It has come in part from a dramatic growth in communications, agricultural productivity, and trade which has meant that a crop failure in one part of the world no longer automatically means unanswered famine and death for those involved. It has come in part from unprecedented expansion of the global economy which has resulted in a progressive decrease in the proportion of humanity—although not as yet a decrease in numbers—living in absolute poverty and unable to produce or purchase the means for their survival, including their health care.

Nils Daulaire, Global Health Council, www.globalhealth.org, April 9, 1999.

It is also important in discussing equity and globalisation to focus on the absolute poverty of nations and of households and not only on poverty relative to the rich. Thus, while some gaps may increase, it may still be the case that poor nations and poor households are getting richer. This is good for them and for their health—even if some nations and households are getting richer and healthier more rapidly.

In summary, globalisation, economic growth, and improvements in health go hand in hand. Economic growth is good for the incomes of the poor, and what is good for the incomes of the poor is good for the health of the poor. Globalisation is a key component of economic growth. Openness to trade and the inflow of capital, technology, and ideas are essential for sustained economic growth.

For a country to isolate itself from the benefits of globalisation is, in general, to condemn its citizens to unnecessary and protracted poverty and misery. Isolationism also allows unscrupulous and oppressive governments to continue to be unscrupulous and oppressive without fear of condemnation or intervention from the outside. Would the campaigns against corruption and government malpractice be as well informed and as strong as they are in the absence of globalisation and information technology? Would Aung San Suu Kyi [leader of the nonviolent movement for human rights and democracy in Burma] still be alive if the rest of the world was not watching her every move? Would genocide in East Timor have been cut short in an unglobalised world? Many very poor people in the world do not have governments that are concerned for their welfare and their interests. Such poor people are given hope by an interconnected world in which information and ideas flow rapidly and protest and action can be mobilised in the face of oppression, corruption, and genocide.

The global movement to improve the rights and prospects of women worldwide, which still has a long way to go, would have nothing like its present moral or practical force in the world in the absence of continuing globalisation. We may lament the tendency for cultural globalisation, although as I travel the world I find that local cultural diversity is alive and well. However, without a trend towards global moral and ethical standards, more Chinese women would still be crippled by foot binding, more African women would still be genitally mutilated, and more Indian women would be killed or beaten in disputes over dowries. Are these advances worth the eyesore of the McDonald's outlet in Hyderabad or a charming market town in rural France? We must each weigh the outcomes.

Bridging the Digital Divide

Technology and its diffusion are another piece of the globalisation story with important implications for health. The pace of technological change is exponential. Ninety per cent of all scientists who have ever lived are alive today. The human genome has been mapped more rapidly than could have been imagined. The explosion of information technology is making it far easier and far cheaper to communicate globally.

In 1930 a three minute telephone call from New York to London cost over $300, today it costs 30 cents.

The previous G8 meeting in Okinawa lamented the digital divide. What is more remarkable is the speed at which information technology has reached low income countries and even quite remote areas within those countries. No previous technological revolution, such as steam engines, electricity, or telephones, has diffused so widely and so quickly. Non-governmental organisations in towns in India or Tanzania are now able to connect with like-minded people around the world, perhaps to organise the next anti-globalisation street protests. In terms of connectivity to the internet, Singapore has overtaken the whole of Europe, South Korea does as well as Britain, and middle and large low income countries are increasing their internet connectivity rapidly. Already 0.5% of Indians (five million people) have online access, and this number is set to rise rapidly during the next five years.

The Health Impact of the Internet

The internet itself will have a substantial health impact in low and middle income countries. There are two reasons for this. Firstly, the internet will promote more rapid economic growth than would otherwise have occurred, and this economic growth, in the presence of sound public policy, will promote better incomes and better health for the poor. There are many pathways by which the internet will boost the economy, all of which essentially mean a greater ability for companies in developing countries, especially small ones, to participate in global trade and commerce. Secondly, the communications, data management, and administrative capacity offered by the internet will greatly improve the management and delivery of healthcare services, the surveillance of communicable disease, the response to epidemics, the monitoring of antibiotic resistance, and a host of other important applications in the health sector. We have not yet begun to see the benefits of this application of information technology in most countries.

The third flaw in the protestors' world view is their lack of a counter proposal. What is the alternative to globalisation and economic growth that we should prefer? Isolationism? The erection or maintenance of national boundaries that inhibit the flow of ideas, technology, and money? Economic stagnation? Luckily, we have no widespread experience of such policies, but we do have local evidence of their virtues. They deliver Myanmar rather than Malaysia, North Korea rather than South Korea, Cuba rather than Costa Rica. Chacun à son goût [Each to his own taste].

The Drawbacks of Globalisation

But every silver lining has a cloud. The shift with development from food scarcity to food surplus is accompanied by rising obesity and its associated health consequences. The steady reduction in mortality rates (until HIV infection and AIDS came along) has allowed people to live long enough to develop unpleasant chronic and degenerative diseases. And so with globalisation. A process that has unquestionably brought benefits to many countries also carries with it risks and negative consequences.

This is not new. Perhaps the most devastating impact of globalisation was the spread of deadly epidemics that accompanied European expansion and colonisation between roughly 1500 and 1800. These epidemics decimated immunologically naïve populations, especially in the Americas and Oceania. Global spread of infection continues today, although (with the notable exception of AIDS) we now have better knowledge and tools with which to ameliorate the consequences.

In addition to the threats from emerging and re-emerging infections that are increased by globalisation, there is the massive debate on global environmental change and its health consequences. I have no doubt that there are grave concerns to be researched and addressed in this area. However, it is noteworthy that the widely held pessimism of the public health community has now been comprehensively challenged.

The protestors derailed the Seattle meeting of the World Trade Organisation and seriously disrupted the G8 summit in Genoa. This despite the fact that matters of vital importance to poor people and to developing countries were being discussed at these meetings. In November [2001] in Doha, the World Trade Organisation's 142 member countries will try to launch a new round of global trade negotiations. On the agenda are agricultural tariffs, an area in which the rich countries are notoriously protectionist. Reaching new international agreements on freer trade, particularly in agriculture, is far more important to the lives of the poor than debt relief. Let the health and medical community worldwide give all support to the World Trade Organisation and to the Doha meeting in the name of poverty alleviation and better health for all.

"Significant unexplained connections remain between death and disability for many diseases . . . that may be filled by 'environment.'"

Pollution Threatens Human Health

John Eyles and Nicole Consitt

According to John Eyles and Nicole Consitt in the following viewpoint, studies show a relationship between air pollution and health problems such as asthma, lung cancer, and heart disease. In addition, the authors contend, modern food production methods expose people to toxins in food and water. Since trade, travel, and migration have linked people worldwide, reducing the risks of environmental hazards will require international cooperation, the authors maintain. Eyles is a geography professor and Consitt a research assistant at McMaster University in Ontario, Canada.

As you read, consider the following questions:

1. According to Eyles and Consitt, why is environmental exposure to contaminants difficult to explain?
2. In the authors' opinion, what fuels the public's perception of the risk of environmental pollution?
3. What two types of environmental hazards does the World Health Organization identify?

How important is the environment when it comes to human health? The 1962 publication *Silent Spring*[1] not only rippled throughout the scientific community and public conscience but initiated a growing wave of research into the linkages between environment and human health. Yet there is limited hard scientific proof that adverse health outcomes are caused by the contaminant load that human activities add to the environment. Most scientists remain concerned about the emerging epidemic of lifestyle diseases and are committed to genetic research as the next magic bullet, while the relations between human health and environmental exposures remain highly contentious.

For example, dichlorodiphenyltrichloroethane (DDT) was indicted as an extreme risk to human health in spite of a significant lack of human toxicological or epidemiological evidence. Despite the chemical's proven ability to control, if not eradicate, the spread of mosquito-borne malaria in human populations, animal studies were deemed sufficient to warrant the ban on the use of DDT-containing agents. But ... research does not support any association between DDE (p,p'-dichlorodiphenyldichloroethylene, the predominant DDT metabolite) and, for example, breast cancer. Whether or not the ban on DDT was premature or in fact beneficial to human health is still debatable. DDT remains a significant part of mosquito-control programs in malaria-endemic countries and undoubtedly saves thousands of lives. . . .

A Contentious Issue

So why worry about the environment? Environmental exposure is difficult to delineate. Scientific evidence to support associations between environmental contaminants and human disease is often limited to very high exposures resulting from occupational or accidental exposures. For the general public, evidence remains circumstantial that what we eat, drink, and breathe are major risk factors for disease. Yet there are significant fears that these factors outside our control adversely affect us, making the environment-health linkage intensely political.

1. a book by Rachel Carson that connected human-made pesticides to human and wildlife health problems

The Skeptical Environmentalist,[2] the . . . antithesis to *Silent Spring*, asserts that the state of the global environment and pollution is improving and refutes much of the research that implies any connection between our environment and human disease. In addition, the physical environment was notably absent as an important factor in WHO's [World Health Organization's] 2003 report, *Social Determinants of Health*. Trying to quantify the disease burden borne by environmental factors is complicated not only by changing definitions and parameters but also by the unknown impacts of emerging risks. One recent study evaluating the role of environmental pollutants on human health stated that only 8–9 percent of the total disease burden is attributable to environmental pollutants, with unsafe water, poor sanitation, and hygiene occupying the most significant sources of exposure along with indoor air pollution. A study that followed looked specifically at the effects of water, sanitation, and hygiene and concluded that these environmental factors accounted for 4 percent of global mortality and 5.7 percent of total disability-adjusted life years.

But despite these statistics, there is still considerable concern regarding environmental influences on human health —not only because these factors are outside the control of individuals, but because there is still so much that science does not know. Significant unexplained connections remain between death and disability for many diseases—cancer, heart disease, diabetes, neurological conditions—that may be filled by "environment.". . .

Furthermore, the interconnectedness of the world through trade, travel, and migration means that risk appears to be democratized, with all the world apparently at risk and little protection from such environmental exposures. The most common public health risks are indeed mundane and thus not newsworthy. High profile outbreaks of infectious disease grab the public's attention and often fuel our risk perceptions. In a recent poll of U.S. voters, 78 percent agreed or strongly agreed that no amount of environmental pollution

2. a book by Bjorn Lomborg that challenges widely held beliefs that the global environment is progressively getting worse

was tolerable if it adversely affected human health. Our most common exposures to risk come from areas over which we seem to have little control: the quality of water, food, and air. Such a perceived glut of risks makes their understanding particularly challenging for the public. What should we worry about? . . .

The Hazards That Threaten Human Health

WHO identifies two sets of hazards that lead to human vulnerability. Traditional hazards are associated with a lack of development: They are related to poverty, lack of access to safe drinking water, inadequate basic sanitation in the household and community, indoor air pollution from cooking and using bio-mass fuel, and inadequate solid waste disposal. Modern hazards are associated with unsustainable development practices and include water pollution from populated areas, industry, and intensive agriculture; urban air pollution from vehicular traffic, coal power stations, and industry; climate change; stratospheric ozone depletion; and transboundary pollution. In a follow-up to its burden of disease report, WHO refines these hazards into risk factors. Of the 26 identified, 6 are environmental: ambient air; indoor air; lead; water, sanitation, and hygiene; climate change; and selected occupational risks.

Many of these hazards, or risk factors, involve several exposure pathways. For example, changes associated with climate and weather and affecting air, water, and animal populations have direct impacts on human health and disease burdens. The World Bank suggests that such change is occurring at unprecedented rates as large quantities of carbon dioxide, methane, and other greenhouse gases continue to be released into the atmosphere, a suggestion confirmed by Intergovernmental Panel on Climate Change summaries of the scientific evidence. Direct effects are primarily altered rates of heat- and cold-related events. For example, the death tolls attributed to heat stress can be surprisingly high. In Chicago in July 1995, heat stress was implicated in the deaths of 726 people during a 4-day heat wave. Some 15,000 are estimated to have died during August's blistering heat in France in 2003. For industrialized countries such as the

United States and Canada, the greatest direct impacts lie in the contribution of greenhouse gases to smog and air pollution and hence respiratory diseases. The indirect effects of

The Environment Is Getting Worse

In the [1990s] in every environmental sector, conditions have either failed to improve, or they are worsening:

Public health. Unclean water, along with poor sanitation, kills over 12 million people each year, most in developing countries. Air pollution kills nearly 3 million more. Heavy metals and other contaminants also cause widespread health problems.

Food supply. Will there be enough food to go around? In 64 of 105 developing countries studied by the UN [United Nations] Food and Agriculture Organization, the population has been growing faster than food supplies. Population pressures have degraded some 2 billion hectares of arable land— an area the size of Canada and the US.

Freshwater. The supply of freshwater is finite, but demand is soaring as population grows and use per capita rises. By 2025, when world population is projected to be 8 billion, 48 countries containing 3 billion people will face shortages.

Coastlines and oceans. Half of all coastal ecosystems are pressured by high population densities and urban development. A tide of pollution is rising in the world's seas. Ocean fisheries are being overexploited, and fish catches are down.

Forests. Nearly half of the world's original forest cover has been lost, and each year another 16 million hectares are cut, bulldozed, or burned. Forests provide over US$400 billion to the world economy annually and are vital to maintaining healthy ecosystems. Yet, current demand for forest products may exceed the limit of sustainable consumption by 25%.

Biodiversity. The earth's biological diversity is crucial to the continued vitality of agriculture and medicine—and perhaps even to life on earth itself. Yet human activities are pushing many thousands of plant and animal species into extinction. Two of every three species is estimated to be in decline.

Global climate change. The earth's surface is warming due to greenhouse gas emissions, largely from burning fossil fuels. If the global temperature rises as projected, sea levels would rise by several meters, causing widespread flooding. Global warming also could cause droughts and disrupt agriculture.

Don Hinrichsen et al., *Population Reports*, Fall 2000.

climate change stem from climate's association with other driving forces of environmental change, including population dynamics, urbanization, and production and consumption patterns. For example, one study, published in 1994, shows how climate variability led to the appearance in humans of hantavirus pulmonary syndrome (a rodent-borne disease) when long-lasting drought was punctuated by heavy rains in the U.S. Southwest. An explosion of rodent numbers enabled the virus to take hold, and when drought returned, rodents sought food in human dwellings, bringing the disease with them. Earlier episodes in China have been associated with increased urbanization and inadequate waste treatment or removal, allowing garbage to proliferate. Urban services and pest control were inadequate, leading to more than 100,000 reported cases in China in the early 1990s. . . .

To better understand the environment–human health link, however, it is useful to examine exposure pathways and media: water, air, and food.

Water and Human Health

For many years, water quality has been regarded as a prime indicator of health and well-being, as it plays a crucial role in determining the cause and transmission of disease. While access to water is vital to human life, it also serves as a ubiquitous pathway for illness and disease. Approximately 10 million people die each year from water-related diseases or inadequate sanitation. Put another way, 4 percent of deaths worldwide are due to poor water systems and inadequate sanitation. However, a WHO Burden of Disease study came to a more conservative estimate, attributing 1.7 million deaths worldwide to unsafe water, sanitation, and hygiene. Global environmental change affects pathogens (such as viruses, bacteria, protozoa, and fungi), vectors, and hosts by influencing their survival, abundance, and dispersal. Waterborne disease outbreaks can be local (in a particular city or village), national, or international in shape. Increased temperatures, flooding, and runoff are some examples that enhance the transmission route of microorganisms to humans.

Water is a significant route for disease transmission, especially in the tropical world: Typhoid fever, cholera, dysentery, enteritis (bacteria), infectious hepatitis (viruses), amoebic dysentery, giardiasis (protozoa), and schistosomiasis (worms) are all transmitted via water. Disease outbreaks and their associated transmission routes that are linked to water can be categorized in the following manner: waterborne (infections spread through water supplies); water-washed (infections spread through lack of water for personal hygiene); water-vectored (infections spread by insects that depend on water); and water-based (infections spread though an aquatic invertebrate host). Most of these are exacerbated by human activities that pollute the water. . . .

Air Quality and Human Health

Environmental exposures often have the most dramatic impacts on our respiratory systems: Although there has been obvious progress made in air quality in developed countries, WHO reports that outdoor air pollution accounts for more than 800,000 deaths a year worldwide. Air pollution affects people outdoors and indoors, at workplaces and in homes. The environmental consequences of air pollution tend to be noticed in haze and reduced visibility. For example, average visibility in Mexico City has been reduced from 11 kilometers to 1.6 kilometers since the late 1940s. Environmental monitoring shows where the worst air quality is found, but much depends on the pollutants that are measured. The U.S. Environmental Protection Agency (EPA) notes that the worst urban areas for ozone nonattainment targets within the United States are the Los Angeles basin; Chicago-Gary, Houston-Galveston, and New York-New Jersey metro areas; and the southeast desert in California.

Because different pollutants have different health effects, what is measured and controlled is important. In general, exposure to low levels of such pollutants as ozone, sulfur oxides, nitrogen oxides, and particulate matter can irritate the eyes and cause inflammation of the respiratory tract. Many air pollutants may also suppress the immune system, increasing susceptibility to infections. Following the nearly 2,500 deaths that occurred in London in December 1952, attention has been focused on particulate matter (PM). In the last 30 years, consistent association has been found between PM and increases in mortality, hospital admissions, and morbidity. . . . In a study of 20 U.S. cities, increases in the relative rate of death from all causes and respiratory and cardiovascular causes were found with each increase in PM level. A detailed study of Montreal found increases in daily mortality and most measures of particulate air pollution of the order of 1–2 percent. While this seems small, it is a serious public health issue on a population level: For example, in cities of more than one million people, 1–2 percent equates to 10,000–20,000 people. . . .

Studies are revealing relationships between air quality and many adverse health outcomes, including asthma, lung cancer, cardiovascular disease, diabetes, stroke, and chronic obstructive pulmonary disease. WHO officials stated in a 2000 Air Quality and Health meeting in Geneva [Switzerland] that overall, air pollution from various sources contributes to 3 million deaths worldwide. Because of the complexities of causation, this is merely an estimate; the actual death toll may be anywhere from 1.4 million to 6 million. Air pollution's influence on chronic morbidity is much more dramatic. . . .

Indoor Air Pollution

Poor indoor air quality is as significant as outdoor or ambient air pollution: Soot from burning wood, dung, crop residues, and coal for cooking and heating affects about 22 million people worldwide, mostly women and girls. Poor indoor air quality is estimated to kill more than 2.2 million people each year, nearly all in developing countries. In countries such as the United States and Canada, indoor air quality is also a growing concern.

The indoors—homes, shopping malls, offices, and factories—is an important environment in which we spend between 50 and 90 percent of our time, depending on age and occupation. Colds, influenza, headaches, and stomach upsets are common illnesses, often associated with common indoor pollutants, including radon, cigarette smoke, carbon monoxide, nitrogen dioxide, formaldehyde, solvents, pesticides, and ozone. Also found indoors are fungi, bacteria, viruses, mites, pollens, and animal dander, all of which can exacerbate ailments, especially in closed, often air-tight buildings. In fact, the epidemic of childhood asthmas is frequently associated with these indoor contaminants. Asthma is the leading chronic illness of children in the United States, responsible for many school absences, hospitalizations, and visits to the emergency room. EPA estimates that 17 million Americans (children and adults) suffer from asthma, costing $7 billion–$9 billion annually in direct and indirect costs. Furthermore, some of the pollutants in indoor air lead to nonrespiratory problems—such as cancer (caused by radon and tobacco smoke)—and reproductive and developmental effects (from lead) and may act as an amplifier of other conditions, particularly heart disease.

Food and Poor Health

The linkage between food consumption, environment, and health is a complex and important one. For example, WHO's 2004 *Inheriting the World: The Atlas of Children's Health and the Environment* gives credence to the importance of safe food as one of the most important preventive measures to protecting children's health. In the developing world, food security is seriously affected by environmental practices, farming styles, water availability, land ownership patterns and the tensions between subsistence and export-based agriculture. Food insecurity can result in malnutrition and illness. . . .

Globally, changes occurring in the environment (pesticides, antibiotics, and the changing balance of animal and insect populations) are translated into the food we eat. A few examples of the increasing links between imported raw fruits and vegetables that weigh heavily in the minds of consumers include a hepatitis A outbreak linked to Mexican green onions, the E. coli and salmonella outbreaks associated with alfalfa sprouts, and the high profile cyclosporiasis outbreak of the late 1990s caused by Guatemalan raspberries. According to the U.S. Centers for Disease Control and Prevention, since 1995 there have been 13 food-borne outbreaks linked to alfalfa sprouts, with 10 of those occurring in the United States.

There are also possible linkages between humans, animals, and disease. Crowding—the result of urbanization—and dense population clusters enable favorable conditions of disease transference and proliferation. In China, Guangdong's population of 80 million people live in close contact with the animals, poultry, and fish they consume. Cross pollution between animals and the close proximity of humans with these animals, increases the ability of viruses to jump species and infect humans. Zoonotic diseases are known to proliferate in overcrowded populations wrought with pollution and unhygienic conditions. . . .

Modern factory farming practices have helped the emergence of antibiotic resistance; outbreaks of food-borne illness and disease; and the contamination of water supplies, degradation of land, and loss of biodiversity. Foods expose us to pesticide residues directly and indirectly—through air and water. Pesticides can be carried through air currents during their application to vegetables and fruit crops, and they can pass into drinking-water supplies through farm runoff.

The bioaccumulation of toxins in the food chain has been known in the scientific community for years. . . . The news media has drawn the public's attention to this increasing threat to human health. Research sampling tissues in Arctic animals first revealed the bioaccumulation of chemical pollutants in the local food chains of relatively nonindustrial regions. Now, however, research is revealing high levels of toxins in food animals farmed in controlled settings, removed from the wild environment. . . .

In some ways, as all these examples attest, dealing with potential environmental insults on health seems even more intractable. Environment impacts human health and well-being at many different scales—from the global, with climate change and trade relations—to the local and personal, with the existence of contaminated communities and the personal impacts of the environment through UV-radiation and food and water consumption. But the apparent pervasiveness of environmental effects suggests we cannot stand still as our own health and that of our children and grandchildren is affected. And in our interconnected world our prosperity and security may also be threatened. The intractability of action and intervention does not imply or mean impossibility. At a macroscale, there is a need for international actions, agreements, and cooperation. The fact that the environment is on the agenda of many wealthy nations means that it will be addressed before long. . . . Only then will environmental concerns be given teeth.

Multinational agreements are hard to engineer. . . . Yet there are good bilateral collaborations to point to, especially the Great Lakes agreements between the United States and Canada, which have resulted . . . in cleaner, safer, and healthier lakes, catchments, and drinking water systems. . . . At the local level, there is need for local cleanups and changes in personal behavior to make our cities and industrial places cleaner and healthier. In all, there is a continued need for monitoring, surveillance, research, and education— the bulwarks of a public health system that protects our health. All these actions, it is hoped, will lead to greater respect for the global commons.

It is now almost trite to say we have one Earth, which we despoil at our peril. But now we recognize the Earth or nature, through our activities, adversely affects humans, redistributing disease and death across space. German astronaut Ulf Merbold said, "For the first time in my life, I saw the horizon as a curved line. It was accentuated by the thin seam of dark blue light—our atmosphere. Obviously, this was not the 'ocean' of air I had been told about so many times in my life. I was terrified by its fragile appearance." The stakes are therefore high for the planet with respect to human activities. Despite the scientific uncertainties in the linkages between environmental exposures and health outcomes, there are serious grounds for concern for human health. In fact, some authorities suggest that such exposures are important mediating factors explaining the relationship between low socioeconomic status and ill-health and premature mortality. Furthermore, agencies such as U.S. Centers for Disease Control and Prevention continue to enhance their monitoring of environmental influences on health. Genetics, lifestyle, and sociodemographics matter and shape health. So, too, does environment, directly, indirectly, and in combination with other factors. And it threatens our most precious resource—our children: More than five million die each year from environment-related conditions. The biggest threats lurk in the places that should be safe—home, school, and community. Thus, striving for a healthy environment matters for our own health and future.

"A large part of humanity is now better nourished [and] less frequently exposed to water-borne pathogens and air pollution."

The Threat That Pollution Poses to Human Health Has Been Exaggerated

Kendra Okonski and Julian Morris

Claims that pollution threatens human health are exaggerated, maintain Kendra Okonski and Julian Morris in the following viewpoint, which has been excerpted from their anthology *Environment & Health: Myths & Realities*. No evidence exists that small amounts of agricultural chemicals cause cancer, they claim. Assertions that global warming will lead to increases in malaria and temperature-related deaths are also unfounded, the authors contend. Okonski and Morris are scholars at the International Policy Network, a British libertarian think tank.

As you read, consider the following questions:

1. In Okonski and Morris's opinion, what are the environmental benefits of some agricultural chemicals?
2. What are some of the concerns that people become distracted from in their obsession with the potential carcinogenic effect of chemicals, in the authors' view?
3. According to the authors, what is the biggest contributor to temperature-related human mortality?

Kendra Okonski and Julian Morris, *Environment & Health: Myths & Realities.* London: International Policy Press, 2004. Copyright © 2004 by the International Policy Network. Reproduced by permission.

Are modern industry and economic activity causing an irreversible decline in the state of the natural environment, leading to ever-worse problems with human health? Are children the unwitting victims of our profligate society? Are we in a 'race to the bottom' that will ultimately lead to the demise of humanity? . . .

In many cases, the science is extremely complex and a simple answer concerning impacts would not be feasible. However, in all cases it is clear that hysteria is unwarranted and that the level of regulatory intervention is either already sufficient or even excessive. . . .

Chemicals in Agriculture and Food

Although we are unaware of any attempts to put pressure on governments to ban water (at least in its unadulterated form), it is one of the few commonly used chemicals that seem to have avoided the accusatory finger of activists.

The same cannot be said for chemicals used in agriculture and foods. Many of these chemicals confer significant benefits to human beings—for example by reducing the cost of food or increasing its shelf life. Some chemicals have even arguably had environmental benefits—for example, chemicals that increase yields mean that more food can be grown on less land, reducing pressure on wild land; meanwhile, chemicals that enable weeds to be killed with minimal tillage reduce the soil erosion that results when land is ploughed.

In spite of these observable benefits, there has been a strong push for regulation of chemicals used in agriculture and food. To some extent one can understand this impetus, since some of the early pesticides were highly ecotoxic, while many early food additives were poisonous in the doses present in food. However, these chemicals were for the most part eliminated from the food chain by the early part of the 20th century—largely through the voluntary actions of companies seeking to avoid harming their customers. As a result, concerns shifted to other issues, such as cancer. Fears were heightened in the 1950s, when tests began to show that, when given in sufficient concentrations, many of the chemicals used in agriculture and food caused cancer in rodents.

However, over time it became clear that a large proportion

of all chemicals, synthetic and natural, are carcinogenic. . . .

Moreover, not all substances that are carcinogenic at high doses will also be carcinogenic at low doses. The body is capable of dealing with certain amounts of certain types of carcinogen, through various process[es]. So, restricting the use of chemicals merely on the basis that they are rodent carcinogens simply doesn't make sense. It is not even clear that we should aim to reduce all such chemicals to the very low levels that are required in most existing regulations. . . .

The Case of Lead

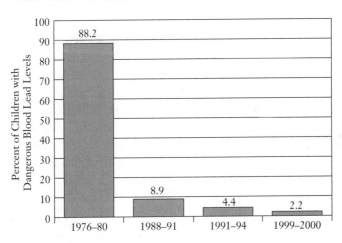

The amounts of toxic chemicals in humans are stable or declining. In the case of lead we now have more than twenty years of data, which show a major decline. In the late 1970s 88 percent of children aged one to five had blood lead levels above the threshold where harm to cognitive development is feared; in the latest data, only 2.2 percent of young children exceed the threshold following a 50 percent decline in . . . ten years.

Steven F. Hayward, American Enterprise Institute, February 25, 2003.

Our obsession with the potential carcinogenic effect of synthetic chemicals used in agriculture and food production has distracted us from these much more important concerns —concerns about what kinds of foods we should eat if we want to obtain the micronutrients that help maintain healthy bodily defences, so that we can deal with the very large number of assaults that are made against our body every day, mostly by natural substances and processes.

The evidence suggests that eating fresh fruit and vegetables helps the human body defend itself from cancer. By contrast, avoiding synthetic agrochemicals present as residues in food does not. So, people who eat less fresh fruit and vegetables because they buy the expensive 'chemical free' varieties are actually harming themselves.

The broader consequences of the anti-scientific attack on the use of synthetic chemicals in food and agriculture are scarier still. What if farmers in poor countries were discouraged or, far worse, prevented from using these technologies in order to ensure that their produce will be acceptable for the over-protected consumers in rich countries? Outputs would fall and they would experience greater uncertainty (one of the huge advantages of synthetic agrochemicals is that it enables much more stable production levels), which would mean less on their own plate as well as lower income. Do we really want our daft obsession with the absurd concept of 'chemical free' food to end up holding back development in poor countries? How does that rest on the conscience of the campaigners against pesticides and other agrochemicals?

Gender Benders?

The evidence amassed by [Bruce] Ames and others has made the chemophobic campaign against supposedly carcinogenic chemical additives increasingly implausible. In response, activists have shifted the debate to new—and equally dubious—territory. In particular, activists have claimed that a variety of chemicals are interfering with the hormone systems of fish, mammals and other animals and, as a result, changing sex ratios, reducing human fertility, and causing cancer.

If these activists had been campaigning against the birth control pill, they might have been on to something. Because, of course, the birth control pill is *intended* to interfere with the hormone system. But even the Pill and various natural oestrogens don't seem to be doing much damage to the human species.

However, the activists are very definitely not talking about the birth control pill. Perhaps this is because they recognise that the Pill is perceived by too many of their constituents to have massive benefits. Perhaps it is because the Pill is not primarily used in agriculture or industry. Whatever the reason, they have chosen a very different target; their target is the same old list of industrial and agricultural chemicals all over again: PCBs, DDE (a breakdown product of DDT) and other 'persistent organic pollutants' (POPs), TCDD (a dioxin), and other industrial and agrochemicals.

Stephen Safe, a professor of Veterinary Physiology & Pharmacology at Texas A&M University, and the director of the Center for Environmental and Rural Health analyses the scientific arguments for the 'endocrine disruption' hypothesis and finds that

> There are no apparent global changes in sperm counts and fertility, rates of hypospadias and cryptorchidism, and birth sex ratios. Testicular cancer is increasing in most countries, but it is not correlated with other indicators of male reproductive capacity. Moreover, testicular cancer is increasing while DDE and other POPs are decreasing, suggesting that exposure to these compounds is not linked to testicular cancer.

While Safe accepts that certain 'endocrine active' chemicals (such as natural oestrogens and perhaps the birth control pill) have adverse effects on fish and wildlife in certain circumstances, the same effects are not observed in humans. Moreover, Safe points out that if we are concerned about human exposure to endocrine disruptors, then we should be more concerned about natural endocrine-disrupting substances than synthetic ones.

Nitrate Nonsense

Dr. Jean-Louis L'hirondel, a practicising doctor in Caen, France, explores claims about nitrates which have been used to justify numerous regulatory directives. Nitrates were previously used as medicines, and were replaced with aspirin and corticoids at the beginning of the 20th century. About thirty years ago, a variety of allegations were made that nitrates cause 'blue-baby syndrome' and exacerbate cancer risks in adults.

L'hirondel's assessment indicates that both claims "lack

scientific basis" based on studies conducted in the last thirty years:

> What causes methaemoglobinaemia in infants is not alimentary nitrates, but nitrites formed in the feeding bottles . . . It has been virtually eradicated in developed countries where people are familiar with basic hygiene rules for preparing bottles of formula milk.

And as stated by the European Commission's Scientific Committee for Food in its 1995 "Opinion on Nitrate and Nitrite":

> Epidemiological studies thus far have failed to provide evidence of a causal association between nitrate exposure and human cancer risk.

Radiation and the No-Threshold Myth of Cancer

In the case of radiation, the "Linear No-Threshold Assumption" has been a "holy mantra", according to which even the lowest, near-zero doses of radiation may cause cancer and genetic harm in human beings. As with other causes of cancer, the linear no-threshold assumption simply does not hold as a general rule.

While the damaging effects of high doses of ionizing radiation are well established, the same is not true for low doses. Dr. Zbigniew Jaworowski of the Central Laboratory for Radiological Protection in Warsaw, Poland, points out that:

> In some areas of the world, natural radiation doses to man and to other biota are many hundreds times higher than the currently accepted dose limits for the general population. No adverse health effects were found in humans, animals and plants in these areas.

Indeed, Jaworowski argues that there are considerable benefits associated with certain uses of low-dose radiation, including medical uses, and there may even be an 'hormetic' effect [i.e., beneficial in low doses while deleterious at high doses]. What is clear is that the current regulated limits of exposure are unnecessarily low:

> During the past several decades there has been a tendency to decrease—to ever-lower values—the exposure dose applied in standards of radiation protection. . . . Justification for such low levels is difficult to conceive, as no one has ever been identifiably injured by radiation while standards set . . . in the

1920s and the 1930s were in force, involving dose levels hundreds or thousands of times higher.

Dr Hans E. Müller, a chemist and physician, and the former director of the Public Health Laboratory in Braunschweig, Germany, shows how an accident in Seveso, Italy, in 1976 was viewed by the world as a tragedy of apocalyptic proportions, confirmation of environmental activists' worst fears, and justification for an enormous number of regulations on dioxin.

The Claims Against Dioxins

The accident at Seveso sadly caused many deaths—of animals. Not one single human being died. In fact, the main human impacts were the relocation of many thousands of people living near the factory, a large number of cases of chloracne—a very unpleasant skin condition—and a much smaller number of more serious, but not fatal, toxic effects.

Müller shows that dioxin "has frequently been the subject of scaremongering by campaigners and others, who claim that it induces cancer", and equally, "the producers of dioxin have sought to counter such fears" so some controversy has erupted over the 'true' impact of dioxin.

Dioxins—a class of chemical compound that includes the feared TCDD—are produced both during natural burning processes and as a result of certain industrial processes. While exposure to certain dioxins at very high concentrations may have negative health consequences, "such concentrations are seldom reached even in exposed and highly contaminated humans". Since humans consume most of their dioxins in the food they eat and since concentrations in food are at levels that are barely detectable, let alone likely to do any harm, it is very unlikely indeed that we are being harmed by dioxin.

Global Warming and Human Health

One of the favourite chestnuts of the modern environmental movement is the fear that we are having a generalized impact on the environment that will come back to haunt us at some stage in the ill-defined distant future in some unspecified way. In an attempt to put some meat on these rather vague bones, some activists have invented stories about mankind being afflicted by various plagues.

A good example of this is the alleged threat of an increase in malaria as a result of global warming. Professor Paul Reiter, a British expert in vector-borne disease and a 22-year veteran of the US Centers for Disease Control, assesses this threat, which rests in large part on the erroneous assumption that malaria is a tropical disease, and finds it wanting.

Reiter discusses the complex history and science of malaria, which was once endemic in Europe but was largely eradicated here during a time of warming temperatures. He notes, however, that Holland—hardly a tropical country—was not certified malaria-free until 1970.

> The story of malaria in Europe is widely known and readily accessible in any good library. Nevertheless, uninformed predictions on the spread of this and other vector-borne diseases to temperate areas are commonplace—even in the scientific literature—and are widely quoted in public discussion of national and international policy on global warming.

Reiter is concerned . . . by focusing on global warming, the world will misprioritise badly-needed policies to eradicate malaria and other vector-borne diseases.

> [No scientist] denies that temperature is a factor in the transmission of mosquito-borne diseases, and that transmission may be affected if the world's climate continues to warm. But it is immoral for political activists to mislead the public by attributing the recent resurgence of these diseases to climate change, particularly in Africa. The true reasons are far more complex, and the principal determinants are politics, economics, and human activities. A creative and organized application of resources to correct the situation is urgently needed, regardless of future climate.

Another human health problem activists are keen to blame on global warming is temperature-related deaths. In the summer of 2003, a heat wave swept through Europe and was the proximate cause of thousands of deaths. Professor Bill Keatinge, Emeritus professor at Queen Mary School of Medicine and Dentistry, University of London, suggests that the actual number of deaths from heat were probably much lower. He shows that although the mortality rate rises during the first two days of a heat wave, this is followed by lower than normal mortality rates. This is probably because many who die are already very ill, and would have died within the following two or three weeks.

Indeed, the reality is that cold temperatures remain the biggest contributor to human mortality. . . .

The Precautionary Principle

Many regulatory actions on environment and health issues . . . have been driven by reliance on the precautionary principle. The World Health Organization also promotes the precautionary principle as the basis of proposed regulatory actions for its members.

The precautionary principle emerged in the late 1960s in response to campaigns by environmentalists to limit the use of new technologies—specifically nuclear power.

As it is currently conceived, the Precautionary Principle (PP) consists of two key components:

1. Reversal of burden of proof: anyone proposing to use a technology must ensure that it is safe before use.
2. Increase in the standard of proof: more rigorous testing of technologies is required before they can be declared 'safe'.

The particular standard depends on which version of the PP is employed—Strong or Weak.

The Strong PP requires absolute safety. Thus Jeremey Leggett, then with Greenpeace, stated in 1990:

> For organizations like Greenpeace, what comes first must be the needs of the environment . . . the modus operandi we would like to see is: "Do not admit a substance unless you have proof that it will do no harm to the environment"—the precautionary principle . . . the fact that proof of harm might come too late—or that proof is invariably hard to demonstrate with absolute certainty—only augments the license given to the polluters.

The Weak PP is more ambiguous about what level of proof is required. Thus, Principle 15 of the Rio Declaration states:

> Where there are threats of serious or irreversible damage, lack of full scientific certainty shall not be used as a reason for postponing cost-effective measures to prevent environmental degradation.

If applied generally, strong PP would shut down civilisation because every technology carries with it unknown risks. Clearly this is impracticable!

The Weak PP, on the other hand, is very vague. But vagueness is not a merit. It enables arbitrary action—including the imposition of restrictions regardless of costs or benefits.

General application of the PP may prevent people from being exposed to some new risks, but it also prevents them from reducing their exposure to existing risks. New technologies generally provide net benefits; if they did not, there would be little incentive to produce them. Examples of such benefits include higher crop yields, speedier communication, better medicine, clean and reliable energy sources, almost no air pollution and better, less polluted, water.

That new technologies have provided net benefits to humanity is obvious from long term trends in available food supplies, infant mortality, access to safe water and sanitation, and life expectancy, all of which have improved remarkably over time. As a result, a large part of humanity is now better nourished, less frequently exposed to water-borne pathogens and air pollution, and less likely to die or suffer ill effects as a result of disease.

"[Genetically modified] foods in general might create unpredicted allergies, toxins, antibiotic resistant diseases, and nutritional problems."

Genetically Modified Food Threatens Human Health

Jeffrey M. Smith

Consuming genetically modified (GM) food exposes people to unknown dangers, maintains Jeffrey M. Smith in the following viewpoint. Inserting foreign genetic material into food DNA may create unknown toxins or allergens, he claims. In fact, Smith contends, soy allergies increased significantly after GM soy was introduced in the United Kingdom. Nevertheless, Smith asserts, GM foods remain unmonitored, creating risks for the millions of people who are eating them. Smith is author of *Seeds of Deception: Exposing Industry and Government Lies About the Safety of the Genetically Engineered Foods You're Eating.*

As you read, consider the following questions:

1. What questions did the U.S. National Academy of Sciences report raise about the blanket approval of GM foods?
2. What do animal studies show about the safety of some GM foods, in the author's opinion?
3. According to the author, what are the implications of the only human GM feeding study ever conducted?

Jeffrey M. Smith, "Genetically Engineered Foods May Pose National Health Risk," www.seedsofdeception.com. Reproduced by permission.

In a study in the early 1990's rats were fed genetically modified (GM) tomatoes. Well actually, the rats refused to eat them. They were force-fed. Several of the rats developed stomach lesions and seven out of forty died within two weeks. Scientists at the FDA [Food and Drug Administration] who reviewed the study agreed that it did not provide a demonstration of reasonable certainty of no harm. In fact, agency scientists warned that GM foods in general might create unpredicted allergies, toxins, antibiotic resistant diseases, and nutritional problems. Internal FDA memos made public from a lawsuit reveal that the scientists urged their superiors to require long-term safety testing to catch these hard-to-detect side effects. But FDA political appointees, including a former attorney for [chemical giant] Monsanto in charge of policy, ignored the scientists' warnings. The FDA does not require safety studies. Instead, if the makers of the GM foods claim that they are safe, the agency has no further questions. The GM tomato was approved in 1994.

Dismissing the Studies

According to a July 27 [2004] report from the US National Academy of Sciences (NAS), the current system of blanket approval of GM foods by the FDA might not detect unintended changes in the composition of the food. The process of gene insertion, according to the NAS, could damage the host's DNA with unpredicted consequences. The Indian Council of Medical Research (ICMR), which released its findings a few days earlier, identified a long list of potentially dangerous side effects from GM foods that are not being evaluated. The ICMR called for a complete overhaul of existing regulations.

The safety studies conducted by the biotech industry are often dismissed by critics as superficial and designed to avoid finding problems. Tragically, scientists who voice their criticism, and those who have discovered incriminating evidence, have been threatened, stripped of responsibilities, denied funding or tenure, or fired. For example, a UK [United Kingdom] government-funded study demonstrated that rats fed a GM potato developed potentially pre-cancerous cell growth, damaged immune systems, partial atrophy of the liver, and inhibited development of their brains, livers and testicles. When the lead scientist went public with his concerns, he was promptly fired from his job after 35 years and silenced with threats of a lawsuit.

Mounting Evidence

Americans eat genetically modified foods every day. Although the GM tomato has been taken off the market, millions of acres of soy, corn, canola, and cotton have had foreign genes inserted into their DNA. The new genes allow the crops to survive applications of herbicide, create their own pesticide, or both. While there are only a handful of published animal safety studies, mounting evidence, which needs to be followed up, suggests that these foods are not safe.

Rats fed GM corn had problems with blood cell formation. Those fed GM soy had problems with liver cell formation, and the livers of rats fed GM canola were heavier. Pigs fed GM corn on several Midwest farms developed false pregnancies or sterility. Cows fed GM corn in Germany died mysteriously. And twice the number of chickens died when fed GM corn compared to those fed natural corn.

Soon after GM soy was introduced to the UK, soy allergies skyrocketed by 50 percent. Without follow-up tests, we can't be sure if genetic engineering was the cause, but there are plenty of ways in which genetic manipulation can boost allergies.

- A gene from a Brazil nut inserted into soybeans made the soy allergenic to those who normally react to Brazil nuts.
- GM soy currently consumed in the US contains a gene from bacteria. The inserted gene creates a protein that was never before part of the human food supply, and might be allergenic.
- Sections of that protein are identical to those found in shrimp and dust mite allergens. According to criteria recommended by the World Health Organization (WHO), this fact should have disqualified GM soy from approval.
- The sequence of the gene that was inserted into soy has inexplicably rearranged over time. The protein it creates is likely to be different than the one intended, and

was never subject to any safety studies. It may be allergenic or toxic.

- The process of inserting the foreign gene damaged a section of the soy's own DNA, scrambling its genetic code. This mutation might interfere with DNA expression or create a new, potentially dangerous protein.
- The most common allergen in soy is called trypsin inhibitor. GM soy contains significantly more of this compared with natural soy.

The only human feeding study ever conducted showed that the gene inserted into soybeans spontaneously transferred out of food and into the DNA of gut bacteria. This has several serious implications. First, it means that the bacteria inside our intestines, newly equipped with this foreign gene, may create the novel protein inside of us. If it is allergenic or toxic, it may affect us for the long term, even if we give up eating GM soy.

A Rush to Increase Profits

In their rush to sell these products, [genetic engineering] companies are failing to perform adequate testing or ensure that plants and animals in the centers of biological diversity are protected from genetic pollution. The displacement, harm, or outright extinction of plants, animals, or microorganisms as a result of their intervention does not concern them. Nor do the long-term effects on human health.

The real motivation of these companies is not to increase the nutritional value of food or feed the world, as they claim, but to increase their profits.

Vandana Shiva, *Tierramérica*, 2001.

The same study verified that the promoter, which scientists attach to the inserted gene to permanently switch it on, also transferred to gut bacteria. Research on this promoter suggests that it might unintentionally switch on other genes in the DNA allergens, toxins, carcinogens, or antinutrients. Scientists also theorize that the promoter might switch on dormant viruses embedded in the DNA or generate mutations.

Unfortunately, gene transfer from GM food might not be limited to our gut bacteria. Preliminary results show that the promoter also transferred into rat organs, after they were fed only a single GM meal.

This is only a partial list of what may go wrong with a single GM food crop. The list for others may be longer. Take for example, the corn inserted with a gene that creates its own pesticide. We eat that pesticide, and plenty of evidence suggests that it is not as benign as the biotech proponents would have us believe. Preliminary evidence, for example, shows that thirty-nine Philippinos living next to a pesticide-producing cornfield developed skin, intestinal, and respiratory reactions while the corn was pollinating. Tests of their blood also showed an immune response to the pesticide. Consider what might happen if the gene that produces the pesticide were to transfer from the corn we eat into our gut bacteria. It could theoretically transform our intestinal flora into living pesticide factories.

GM corn and most GM crops are also inserted with antibiotic resistant genes. The ICMR, along with the American Medical Association, the WHO, and organizations worldwide, have expressed concern about the possibility that these might transfer to pathogenic bacteria inside our gut. They are afraid that it might create new, antibiotic resistant superdiseases. The defense that the biotech industry used to counter these fears was that the DNA was fully destroyed during digestion and therefore no such transfer of genes was possible. The human feeding study described above, published in February 2004, overturned this baseless assumption.

A Public Unaware

No one monitors human health impacts of GM foods. If the foods were creating health problems in the US population, it might take years or decades before we identified the cause. One epidemic in the 1980's provides a chilling example. A new disease was caused by a brand of the food supplement L-tryptophan, which had been created through genetic modification and contained tiny traces of contaminants. The disease killed about 100 Americans and caused sickness or disability in about 5–10,000 others. The only reason that doctors were able to identify that an epidemic was occurring, was because the disease had three simultaneous characteristics: it was rare, acute, and fast acting. Even then it was nearly missed entirely.

Studies show that the more people learn about GM foods, the less they trust them. In Europe, Japan, and other regions, the press has been far more open about the potential dangers of genetic manipulation. Consequently, consumers there demand that their food supply be GM-free and manufacturers comply. But in the US, most people believe they have never eaten a GM food in their lives (even though they consume them daily). Lacking awareness, complacent consumers have been the key asset for the biotech industry in the US. As a result, millions of Americans are exposed to the potential dangers, and children are most at risk. Perhaps the revelations in the reports released on opposite sides of the planet will awaken consumers as well as regulators, and GM foods on the market will be withdrawn.

> *"Transgenic technology holds the potential to increase food production, reduce the use of synthetic chemical pesticides, and actually make foods safer and healthier."*

Genetically Modified Food Will Improve Human Health

Gregory Conko and C.S. Prakash

In the following viewpoint Gregory Conko and C.S. Prakash claim that genetically modified crops can feed the hungry and improve human health. Transgenic plants that resist insects and plant diseases can improve agricultural productivity in the developing world, where the risk of food scarcity is greatest, the authors maintain. In addition, the authors assert, biotechnology can enhance the nutritional value of plants, reducing global malnutrition. Conko and Prakash are cofounders of AgBioWorld Foundation, an organization that promotes agricultural biotechnology.

As you read, consider the following questions:

1. According to Conko and Prakash, why did some Brazilian farmers decide to grow transgenic crops?
2. How do transgenic crops protect farmers from pesticide poisoning, in the authors' opinion?
3. In the authors' view, why have many governments blocked commercialization of biotech foods?

Gregory Conko and C.S. Prakash, "Battling Hunger with Biotechnology," *Economic Perspectives*, vol. 7, May 1, 2002. Copyright © 2002 by the Competitive Enterprise Institute. All rights reserved. Reproduced by permission.

During the coming decades the world will face the extraordinary challenge of conquering poverty and achieving genuine food security with a very potent new tool: agricultural biotechnology. Skeptics argue that transgenic plants represent a vast new threat to both the environment and human health. However, that view is not supported by the overwhelming weight of scientific evidence that has been generated over the last three decades. Furthermore, such criticism ignores the fact that needless restrictions on biotechnology could endanger our ability to battle hunger in the 21st century.

Transgenic technology holds the potential to increase food production, reduce the use of synthetic chemical pesticides, and actually make foods safer and healthier. These advances are critical in a world where natural resources are finite and where one-and-a-half billion people suffer from hunger and malnutrition. Already, farmers in the United States, Canada, and elsewhere have benefited from improvements in productivity and reduced use of synthetic pesticides. But the real future of biotechnology lies in addressing the special problems faced by farmers in less developed nations.

Critics like to dismiss such claims as nothing more than corporate public relations puffery. However, while most commercially available biotech plants were designed for farmers in the industrialized world, the increasing adoption of transgenic varieties by developing countries over the past few years has been remarkable. According to the International Service for the Acquisition of Agri-Biotech Applications (ISAAA), farmers in less developed countries now grow nearly one-quarter of the world's transgenic crops on more than 26 million acres (10.7 million hectares), and they do so for many of the same reasons that farmers in industrialized nations do.

Productivity Gains from Transgenic Crops

Among the most important limiting factors in developing world agricultural productivity is biotic stress from insects, weeds, and plant diseases. Transgenic modifications common in several industrialized nations target these same problems and can be easily transferred into local varieties to help poor farmers in the developing world. For example, South African farmers are already growing transgenic pest-resistant maize, and [in 2002] began planting transgenic soy. South African and Chinese farmers have been growing transgenic insect-resistant cotton for several years, and the Indian government approved it for commercial cultivation in the spring of 2002. This transgenic cotton, similar to the varieties so popular in the United States, is expected to boost yields by 30 percent or more for Indian farmers, according to a recent article in the *Economic Times*. It could even transform India from the world's third largest producer of cotton into the largest.

Globally, transgenic varieties are now grown on more than 109 million acres (44.2 million hectares) in Argentina, Australia, Canada, Chile, China, Mexico, South Africa, and the United States, according to ISAAA. They are even grown on substantial amounts of acreage in Brazil, where no transgenic varieties have yet been approved for commercial cultivation. Farmers there looked across the border and saw how well their Argentine neighbors were doing with transgenic varieties, and smuggling of transgenic soybean seed became rampant. The European Union's (EU) Directorate General for Agriculture estimates that Brazil is now the fifth largest grower of transgenic crops.

Meeting Environmental Goals

Although this first generation of crops was designed primarily to improve farming efficiency, the environmental benefits these crops offer are extensive. The U.S. Department of Agriculture found that U.S. farmers growing transgenic pest-resistant cotton, maize, and soy reduced the total volume of insecticides and herbicides they sprayed by more than 8 million pounds per year. Similar reductions have been seen in Canada with transgenic rapeseed, according to the Canola Council of Canada.

In less developed nations where pesticides are typically sprayed on crops by hand, transgenic pest-resistant crops have had even greater benefits. In China, for example, some 400 to 500 cotton farmers die every year from acute pesticide poisoning. A study conducted by researchers at Rutgers University in the United States and the Chinese Academy of Sciences found that adoption of transgenic cotton varieties in China has lowered the amount of pesticides used by more than 75 percent and reduced the number of pesticide poisonings by an equivalent amount. Another study by economists at the University of Reading in Britain found that South African cotton farmers have seen similar benefits.

The reduction in pesticide spraying also means that fewer natural resources are consumed to manufacture and transport the chemicals. Researchers at Auburn University and Louisiana State University in the United States found that, in 2000 alone, U.S. farmers growing transgenic cotton used 2.4 million fewer gallons of fuel, 93 million fewer gallons of water, and were spared some 41,000 10-hour days needed to apply pesticide sprays.

How to Develop Valuable Biotechnology Research

The following indicator of measuring the value of development efforts proposed by Mahatma Gandhi is the most meaningful yardstick for determining priorities in scientific research designed to help in meeting basic human needs: *"Recall the face of the poorest and the weakest man whom you have seen, and ask yourself if the steps you contemplate are going to be of any use to him. Will he gain anything by it? Will it restore to him control over his own life and destiny?"*

If biotechnology research can be promoted keeping in mind the guideline Gandhi gave, it will become a powerful tool in ensuring sustainable food security in the world.

M.S. Swaminathan, "Genetic Engineering and Food Security: Ecological and Livelihood Issues" in *Agricultural Biotechnology and the Poor*, G.J. Persley and M.M. Lantin, eds., 2000.

Transgenic herbicide-tolerant crops have promoted the adoption of farming practices that reduce tillage or eliminate it altogether. Low-tillage practices can decrease soil erosion by up to 90 percent compared to conventional cultivation, saving valuable topsoil, improving soil fertility, and dramatically reducing sedimentation in lakes, ponds, and waterways.

The productivity gains generated by transgenic crops provide yet another important environmental benefit: they could save millions of hectares of sensitive wildlife habitat from being converted into farmland. The loss and fragmentation of wildlife habitats caused by agricultural development in regions experiencing the greatest population growth are widely recognized as among the most serious threats to biodiversity. Thus, increasing agricultural productivity is an essential environmental goal, and one that would be much easier in a world where agricultural biotechnology is in widespread use.

Opponents of biotechnology argue that organic farming can reduce pesticide use even more than transgenic crops can. But as much as 40 percent of crop productivity in Africa and Asia and about 20 percent in the industrialized countries of North America and Europe are lost to insect pests, weeds, and plant diseases. Organic production methods would only exacerbate those crop losses. There is no way for organic farming to feed a global population expected to grow to 8 or 9 billion people without having to bring substantially more land into agricultural use.

Fortunately, many transgenic varieties that have been created specifically for use in less developed nations will soon be ready for commercialization. Examples include insect-resistant rice varieties for Asia, virus-resistant sweet potato for Africa, and virus-resistant papaya for Caribbean nations. The next generation of transgenic crops now in research labs around the world is poised to bring even further productivity improvements for the poor soils and harsh climates that are characteristic of impoverished regions.

Scientists have already identified genes for resistance to environmental stresses common in tropical nations, including tolerance to soils with high salinity and to those that are particularly acidic or alkaline. Other transgenic varieties can tolerate temporary drought conditions or extremes of heat and cold.

Ensuring Worldwide Food Security

Biotechnology also offers hope of improving the nutritional benefits of many foods. Among the most well known is the variety called "Golden Rice," genetically enhanced with added beta carotene, which is converted to vitamin A in the human body. Another variety developed by the same research team has elevated levels of digestible iron.

The diet of more than 3 billion people worldwide includes inadequate levels of essential vitamins and minerals, such as vitamin A and iron. Deficiency in just these two micronutrients can result in severe anemia, impaired intellectual development, blindness, and even death. And even though charities and aid agencies such as the United Nations Childrens' Fund and the World Health Organization have made important strides in reducing vitamin A and iron deficiency, success has been fleeting. No permanent effective strategy has yet been devised, but Golden Rice may finally provide one.

Importantly, the Golden Rice project is a prime example of the value of extensive public sector and charitable research activities. The rice's development was funded mainly by the New York–based Rockefeller Foundation, which has promised to make the rice available to poor farmers at little or no cost. It was created by scientists at public universities in Switzerland and Germany with assistance from the Philippines-based International Rice Research Institute (IRRI) and from several multinational corporations.

Golden Rice is not the only example. Scientists at publicly funded, charitable, and corporate research centers are developing such crops as cassava, papaya, and wheat with built-in resistance to common plant viruses; rice that can more efficiently convert sunlight and carbon-dioxide for faster growth; potatoes that produce a vaccine against hepatitis B; bananas that produce a vaccine against cholera; and countless others. One lab at Tuskegee University is enhancing the level of dietary protein in sweet potatoes, a common staple crop in sub-Saharan Africa.

The Primary Causes of Hunger

Admittedly, experts recognize that the problem of hunger and malnutrition is not currently caused by a global shortage of food. The primary causes of hunger in recent decades have been political unrest and corrupt governments, poor transportation and infrastructure, and, of course, poverty. All of these problems and more must be addressed if we are to ensure real, worldwide food security. But producing enough for 8 or 9 billion people will require greater yields in the regions where food is needed most, and transgenic crops are good, low-input tools for achieving this.

Although the complexity of biological systems means that some promised benefits of biotechnology are many years away, the biggest threat that hungry populations currently face are restrictive policies stemming from unwarranted public fears. Although most Americans tend to support agricultural biotechnology, many Europeans and Asians have been far more cautious. Anti-biotechnology campaigners in both industrialized and less developed nations are feeding this ambivalence with scare stories that have led to the adoption of restrictive policies. Those fears are simply not supported by the scores of peer-reviewed scientific reports or the data from tens of thousands of individual field trials.

Mankind has been modifying the genetic makeup of plants for thousands of years, often in ways that could have had adverse environmental impacts and that routinely introduced entirely new genes, proteins, and other substances into the food supply. Food-grade tomatoes and potatoes are routinely bred from wild varieties that are toxic to human beings, for example. But plant breeders, biologists, and farmers have identified methods to keep potentially dangerous plants from entering the food chain.

Fears Lead to Needless Regulations

The evidence clearly shows there is no difference between the practices necessary to ensure the safety of transgenic plants and the safety of conventional ones. In fact, because more is known about the genes that are moved in transgenic breeding methods, ensuring the safety of transgenic plants is actually easier. But the public's reticence about transgenic plants has resulted in extensive regulations that require literally thousands of individual safety tests that are often duplicative and largely unnecessary for ensuring environmental protection or consumer safety. In the end, over-cautious rules result in hyperinflated research and development costs and make it harder for poorer countries to share in the benefits of biotechnology.

Perhaps more importantly, restrictions on transgenic plants and onerous labeling requirements for biotech foods have caused many governments to block commercialization —not out of health or environmental concerns but because of a legitimate fear that important European markets could be closed to their exports. As [the 2001] United Nations Development Report acknowledged, opposition by European consumers and very strict legal requirements in European Union member nations have held back the adoption of transgenic crops in underdeveloped nations that need them.

Furthermore, the Cartagena Protocol on Biosafety, adopted in January 2000, will tend to reinforce these counterproductive policies because it permits governments to erect unwarranted restrictions based on the Precautionary Principle, the notion that even hypothetical risks should be enough to keep new products off the market, regardless of their potential benefits. Thus, EU nations can restrict imports of transgenic crops from both industrialized and less developed nations, no matter how much scientific data have been presented showing them to be safe, because opponents can always hypothesize yet another novel risk.

Admittedly, advocates have to take the public's concerns more seriously. Better sharing of information and a more forthright public dialogue are necessary to explain why scientists are confident that transgenic crops are safe. No one argues that we should not proceed with caution, but needless restrictions on agricultural biotechnology could dramatically slow the pace of progress and keep important advances out of the hands of people who need them. This is the tragic side effect of unwarranted concern.

An Important Development Tool

Ultimately, biotechnology is more than just a new and useful agricultural tool. It could also be a hugely important instrument of economic development in many poorer regions of the globe. By making agriculture more productive, labor and resources could be freed for use in other areas of economic growth in nations where farming currently occupies 70 or 80 percent of the population. This, in turn, would be an important step in the journey toward genuine food security.

The choice is clear. Innovators must proceed with due caution. But as a report jointly published by the United

Kingdom's Royal Society, the National Academies of Science from Brazil, China, India, Mexico, and the United States, and the Third World Academy of Science contends: "It is critical that the potential benefits of [transgenic] technology become available to developing countries." It is also critical that industrialized countries not stand in their way.

Periodical Bibliography

The following articles have been selected to supplement the diverse views presented in this chapter.

Erica Barks-Ruggles	"The Globalization of Disease: When Congo Sneezes, Will California Get a Cold?" *Brookings Review*, Fall 2001.
Gregory Conko and Henry I. Miller	"The Toxic Politics of Biotech," *Tech Central Station*, October 6, 2004.
Robert Coplan	"Genetically Modified Food Protests Ignore History, Science," *Baltimore Daily Record*, February 14, 2005.
Council on Foreign Relations	"Genetically Modified Foods Can Feed the World's Hungry," press release, June 20, 2002. www.cfr.org.
Nigole Dyer	"Techno Food: Genetically Modified Crops Cook Up a Sizzling Debate," *Science World*, November 26, 2001.
Nicholas Eberstadt	"The Future of AIDS," *Foreign Affairs*, November/December 2002.
Paul Farmer	"AIDS as a Global Emergency," *Bulletin of the World Health Organization*, October 2003.
Anthony S. Fauci	"The AIDS Epidemic: Considerations for the Twenty-First Century," *New England Journal of Medicine*, September 30, 1999.
Forbes	"Why 'Frankenfood' Is Our Friend," December 11, 2000.
Sarah Hagedorn	"AIDS Orphans in Sub-Saharan Africa: A Looming Threat to Future Generations," *Nieman Reports*, Fall 2004.
Richard L. Harris and Melinda J. Seid	"Globalization and Health in the New Millennium," *Perspectives on Global Development & Technology*, 2004.
Princeton N. Lyman and Greg Behrman	"The Global AIDS Threat," *Dallas Morning News*, July 31, 2004.
Paul Magnusson	"Globalization Is Great—Sort Of," *Business Week*, April 25, 2005.
Phi Kappa Phi Forum	"Protecting the Nation's Health in an Era of Globalization: An Introduction," *Phi Kappa Phi Forum*, Fall 2003.
Adam Piore et al.	"What Green Revolution?" *Newsweek*, September 15, 2003.

Mark W. Rosegrant and Sarah A. Cline	"Global Food Security: Challenges and Policies," *Science*, December 12, 2003.
Devinder Sharma	"Frankenfoods: Slouching Towards the Apocalypse," Organic Consumers Association, May 17, 2003. www.organicconsumers.org.
Vandana Shiva	"Genetic Engineering Threatens Life," *Tierramérica*, 2001.
Bradley T. Smith	"The Biosecurity of Nations," *Foreign Policy*, July/August 2004.
Shamillah Wilson	"The Virus That Follows Vulnerability," *LOLApress*, November 2002.

CHAPTER 3

How Will the Human Impact on the Environment Affect Humanity's Future?

Chapter Preface

One of several debates over the future of humanity's relationship with the environment is whether the shrinking freshwater supply will lead to international conflicts. Experts maintain that as the population increases, the freshwater supply decreases. "Although the 6.3 billion people on earth today use only about 54 percent of the runoff that becomes readily available each year, those figures are expected to rise to 7.8 billion and 70 percent by 2025," claim authors Jen Joynt and Marshall T. Poe. However, the problem is not worldwide water scarcity itself, they argue, but that the available water is unevenly distributed. "Forty-three countries fall below the internationally recognized benchmark of 'water sufficiency': 1,700 cubic meters per person per year. Twenty-nine of those countries experience 'water scarcity,' meaning a supply of less than 1,000 cubic meters per person." What concerns some analysts is that many of these countries are in Asia, Africa, and the Middle East, regions that some assert are already politically unstable. These commentators believe that water scarcity will increase tension in these areas and thus the likelihood of conflict. Others argue that the threat of water scarcity will have the effect of uniting humanity.

Those who believe that water scarcity will lead to conflict cite the tension created when some countries channel water for their own use at the expense of neighboring nations. For example, Israel has mined water in the surrounding area, tasking water systems in neighboring Syria and Jordan. Bangladesh, which depends for its water on rivers that originate in India, is suffering because India has diverted and dammed these water sources. In Africa, Namibian plans to construct a pipeline to divert water from the shared Okavango River have strained relations with its neighbor Botswana. Although Egypt depends on the waters of the Nile for irrigation and power, Ethiopia plans to take more water from the Nile before it reaches Egypt. Experts also predict that falling water tables in the North China Plain and northwest India's Punjab region have created "a highly combustible imbalance between available water supplies and human needs," journalist Ginger Otis maintains. At a 2002 international security conference, experts at the Royal United Services Institute for Defence Studies warned that in Africa, the Middle East, Northern China, and much of Asia, a shortage of water could lead to instability and ultimately armed conflict.

Others contend that there is no evidence that water scarcity will lead to conflict. In fact, they claim, water disputes tend to force countries to cooperate rather than go to war. "I have seen sovereign states and ethnic groups within nations go to war over every resource—oil, land, humans, diamonds, gas, livestock, or gold—but never, interestingly, over renewable resources, and never, in particular, over water development and dams," claims Kader Asmal, South Africa's Minister of Education and member of the World Water Commission. "Indeed, just as rain does not start but rather cools and suppresses fire," Asmal maintains, "so water, by its very nature, tends to induce even hostile co-riparian [river-sharing] countries to co-operate. . . . The weight of historical evidence demonstrates that organized political bodies have signed 3600 water related treaties since A.D. 805." Asmal concludes, "Water is for conserving. Water is for bathing. Water is for drinking. Water is for sharing. Water is the catalyst for peace."

Whether water scarcity will lead to conflict or will unite humanity remains the subject of debate. The authors in the following chapter share their views on other questions concerning the future of humanity's relationship with the environment.

"I have witnessed major climate-driven changes across five continents, changes that are leaving millions homeless, destitute and in danger."

Global Warming Is a Serious Threat to Humanity's Future

Mark Lynas

Most scientists agree that the planet is warming, claims Mark Lynas in the following viewpoint. He argues that humanity's future is at risk unless all nations agree to reduce greenhouse gas emissions, the principal cause of global warming. In Alaska, Lynas asserts, Eskimo villagers are going hungry because global warming has changed the migration patterns of seals and walruses, an important part of the Eskimo diet. In other parts of the world, he maintains, flooding, drought, and sea-level rise are forcing people to leave their homes, creating environmental refugees. Lynas is author of the book *High Tide: News from a Warming World.*

As you read, consider the following questions:

1. According to Lynas, how do some residents of Fairbanks, Alaska, describe global warming?
2. What happened on the island of Funafuti, in the author's view?
3. In the author's opinion, what would be a good start in the effort to reduce greenhouse gas emissions?

Mark Lynas, "It's Later than You Think," *New Statesman*, vol. 132, June 30, 2003. Copyright © 2003 by New Statesman Ltd. Reproduced by permission.

Hardly anyone realises it, but the debate about climate change is over. Scientists around the world have now amassed an unassailable body of evidence to support the conclusion that a warming of our planet—caused principally by greenhouse gas emissions from burning fossil fuel—is under way.

The dwindling band of climate "sceptics", a rag-tag bunch of oil and coal industry frontmen, retired professors and semi-deranged obsessives, is now on the defensive. . . .

The Signs

Meanwhile the world as we once knew it is beginning to unravel. The signs are everywhere, even in Britain. Horse chestnut, oak and ash trees are coming into leaf more than a week earlier than two decades ago. The growing season now lasts almost all year round: in 2000 there were just 39 official days of winter.

Destructive winter floods are part of this warming trend, while in lowland England snow has become a thing of the past. Where I live in Oxford, six out of the past ten winters have been completely snowless—something that happened only twice during the whole 30-year period between 1960 and 1990. The rate of warming has now become so rapid that it is equivalent to your garden moving south by 20 metres every single day.

In other parts of the world, the signs of global warming are more dramatic. . . . Researching a book on the subject, I have witnessed major climate-driven changes across five continents, changes that are leaving millions homeless, destitute and in danger.

The Impact in Alaska

In Alaska I spent a week in the Eskimo village of Shishmaref, on the state's remote western coast, just 70 miles from the eastern coast of Russia. While the midnight sun shone outside, I listened as the village elder, Clifford Weyiouanna, told me how the sea, which used to freeze in October, was now ice-free until Christmas. And even when the sea ice does eventually form, he explained, it is so thin that it is dangerous to walk and hunt on. The changing seasons are also affecting the animals: seals and walruses—still crucial elements of the Eskimo diet—are migrating earlier and are almost impossible to catch. The whole village caught only one walrus last year [2002], after covering thousands of miles by boat.

Shishmaref lives in perpetual fear. The cliffs on which the 600-strong community sits are thawing, and during the last big storm 50 feet of ground was lost overnight. People battled 90-mph winds to save their houses from the crashing waves.

I stood on the shoreline a year ago [in 2002] with Robert Iyatunguk, the co-ordinator of the Shishmaref Erosion Coalition, looking up at a house left hanging over the cliff-top. "The wind is getting stronger, the water is getting higher, and it's noticeable to everybody in town," he told me. "It just kind of scares you inside your body and makes you wonder exactly when the big one is going to hit." In July 2002 the residents voted to abandon the site altogether—a narrow barrier island that has been continuously occupied by Eskimos for centuries—and move elsewhere.

In Fairbanks, Alaska's main town in the interior, everyone talks about warming. The manager of the hostel where I stayed, a keen hunter, told me how ducks had been swimming on the river in December (it's supposed to freeze over in autumn), how bears had become so confused they didn't know whether to hibernate or stay awake, and that winter temperatures, which used to plummet to 40 degrees below zero, now barely touched 25 below.

All around the town, roads are buckling and houses sagging as the permafrost underneath them thaws. In one house, the occupants, a cleaning lady and her daughter, showed me that to walk across the kitchen meant going uphill (the house was tilting sideways) and how shelves had to be rebalanced with bits of wood to stop everything falling off. Other dwellings have been abandoned. New ones are built on adjustable stilts.

Signs in the East

Scientists have long predicted that global warming will lead in some places to intense flooding and drought. When I visited China in April [2002], the country's northern provinces were in the grip of the worst drought in more than a century.

Entire lakes had dried up, and in many places sand dunes were advancing across the farmers' fields.

One lakeside village in Gansu Province, just off the old Silk Road, was abandoned after the waters dried up—apart from one woman, who lives amid the ruins with a few chickens and a cow for company. "Of course I'm lonely!" she cried in answer to my rather insensitive question. "Can you imagine how boring this life is? I can't move; I can do nothing. I have no relatives, no friends and no money." She was tormented by memories of how it had once been, when neighbours had chatted and swapped stories late into the evenings, before the place became a ghost town.

Minutes after I had left, a dust storm blew in. These storms are getting more frequent, and even Beijing is now hit repeatedly every spring. During an earlier visit to a remote village in eastern Inner Mongolia, not far from the ruins of Kubla Khan's fabled Xanadu, I experienced an even stronger storm. Day was turned into night as a blizzard of sand and dust scoured the mud-brick buildings. I cowered inside one house with a Mongolian peasant family, sharing rice wine and listening to tales of how the grass had once grown waist-high on the surrounding plains. Now the land is little more than arid desert, thanks to persistent drought and overgrazing. The storm raged for hours. When it eased in the late afternoon and the sun appeared again, the village cockerels crowed, thinking that morning had come early.

The drought in north-west China is partly caused by shrinking run-off from nearby mountains, which because of the rising temperatures are now capped with less snow and ice than before. Glacier shrinkage is a phenomenon repeated across the world's mountain ranges, and I also saw it at first hand in Peru, standing dizzy with altitude sickness in the high Andes 5,200 metres above the capital, Lima, where one of the main water-supplying glaciers has shrunk by more than a kilometre during the past century.

A Threat to Freshwater Supplies

A senior manager of Lima's water authority told me later how melting ice is now a critical threat to future freshwater supplies: this city of seven million is the world's second-largest desert metropolis after Cairo, and the mountains supply all its water through coastal rivers that pour down from the ice fields far above. It is the snows that keep the rivers running all year round—once the glaciers are gone, the rivers will flow only in the wet season. The same problem afflicts the Indian subcontinent: overwhelmingly dependent on the mighty Ganges, Indus and Brahmaputra rivers that flow from the Himalayas, hundreds of millions of people will suffer water shortages as their source glaciers decline over the coming century.

Global Warming Will Worsen Heat Waves, Increasing Urban Death Rates in the United States

City	1997 climate deaths	2020 climate average deaths*	2050 climate average deaths*
Baltimore, Md.	84	89	140
Chicago, Ill.	191	401	497
Cincinnati, Ohio	14	52	67
Detroit, Mich.	110	163	180
Indianapolis, Ind.	36	56	70
Kansas City, Mo.	49	115	127
Los Angeles, Calif.	68	93	118
Newark, N.J.	26	122	146
Philadelphia, Pa.	129	214	349
Tampa, Fla.	28	64	81
St. Louis, Mo.	79	160	185
Dallas, Texas	36	51	72

* Number derived from averages from three models—United Kingdom Meteorological Model, Global Fluid Dynamics Laboratory Model and Max Planck Institute for Meteorology Model population—and metropolitan areas standardized to current levels. Lives spared due to warmer winters estimated to be negligible.

Sierra Club, November 2000.

Unless alternative water supplies can be secured, Lima will be left depopulated, its people scattered as environmental refugees. This is a category already familiar to the residents of Tuvalu, a group of nine coral atolls in the middle of the Pacific. Tuvalu, together with Kiribati, the Maldives and many other island nations, has made its plight well known to the world community, and an evacuation plan—shifting 75 people each year to New Zealand—is already under way.

I saw at first hand how the islands are already affected by the rising sea level, paddling in knee-deep floodwaters during last year's spring tides, which submerged much of Funafuti and almost surrounded the airstrip. Later that same evening the country's first post-independence prime minister, Toaripi Lauti, told me of his shock at finding his own crop of pulaka (a root vegetable like taro, grown in sunken pits) dying from saltwater intrusion. He recalled how everyone had awoken one morning a few years previously to find that one of the islets on the atoll's rim had disappeared from the horizon, washed over by the waves, its coconut trees smashed and destroyed by the rising sea.

However severe these unfolding climate-change impacts seem, they are—like the canary in the coal mine—just the first whispers of the holocaust that lies ahead if nothing is done to reduce greenhouse gas emissions. Scientists meeting under the banner of the UN [United Nations]-sponsored Intergovernmental Panel on Climate Change (IPCC) have predicted a warming during this century alone of up to six degrees Celsius, which would take the earth into dangerous uncharted waters. [In June 2003] scientists at the UK's [United Kingdom's] Hadley Centre reported that the warming might be even greater because of the complexities of the carbon cycle.

The IPCC's worst-case forecast of six degrees could prove almost unimaginably catastrophic. It took only six degrees of warming to spark the end-Permian mass extinction 251 million years ago, the worst crisis ever to hit life on earth (expertly chronicled by Michael Benton in *When Life Nearly Died*), which led to the deaths of 95 per cent of all species alive at the time.

Reducing Emissions

If humanity is to avoid a similar fate, global greenhouse gas emissions need to be brought down to between 60 and 80 per cent below current levels—precisely the reverse of emissions forecasts recently produced by the International Energy Agency. A good start would be the ratification and speedy implementation of the Kyoto Protocol, which should be superseded after the following decade by the "contraction and convergence" model proposed by the Global Commons Institute in London (www.gci.org.uk), allocating equal per-person emissions rights among all the world's nations.

In the meantime, a network of campaigning groups is currently mobilising under the banner of "No new oil", demanding an end to the exploration and development of new fossil fuel reserves, on the basis that current reserves alone include enough oil, coal and gas utterly to destabilise the world's climate. Searching for more is just as illogical as it is wasteful.

Avoiding dangerous climate change and other large-scale environmental crises will need to become the key organising principle around which societies evolve. All the signs are that few in power realise this—least of all the current US administration, which has committed itself to a policy of wanton destructiveness, with control and exploitation of oil supplies a central theme.

We must abandon the old mindset that demands an oil-based economy, not just because it sparks wars and terrorism, but because the future of life on earth depends on leaving it behind.

"Much of global warming theory is based on global warming computer models that . . . have consistently failed to adequately predict changes in climate."

Claims That Global Warming Is a Threat Are Misleading

Myron Ebell

According to Myron Ebell in the following viewpoint, claims about the threat of global warming are misleading. Public attitudes toward global warming are not based on conclusive research, he argues, but assertions made by global warming alarmists who hope to influence public policy. In fact, Ebell asserts, many global warming claims remain hotly contested. Scientists dispute, for example, whether human activities cause global warming, and whether tropical diseases are increasing due to global warming, he maintains. Ebell is director of Global Warming Policy at the Competitive Enterprise Institute, a libertarian think tank.

As you read, consider the following questions:
1. In Ebell's view, what evidence shows that the last century was not necessarily the warmest in a millennium?
2. What accounts for the perception that storms are more frequent or more intense, in the author's opinion?
3. According to the author, what are some of the positive impacts of global warming?

Universities and government institutions around the world are engaged in an enormous amount of scientific research on global climate change. This research involves not only the various specialized disciplines that study the atmosphere and the temperature record, but also solar physics, oceanography, botany, glaciology, paleo-climatology, and other related subjects. Yet the major impact of this research on the public policy debate over global warming does not come directly from the research itself. Instead, the United Nations' Intergovernmental Panel on Climate Change (IPCC) issues reports summarizing and interpreting recent climate research. The IPCC's official pronouncements are touted by the media and become part of conventional wisdom. The problem is that the IPCC is driven by political goals, which puts a consistent slant on everything it produces. Consequently, its public pronouncements are usually misleading and often inaccurate.

The IPCC Process

Over the past decade, the IPCC has prepared three Assessment Reports which summarize and evaluate the entire range of recent climate research. The Third Assessment Report (or TAR) was published in 2001 by Cambridge University Press in three huge volumes, one for each of the IPCC's three Working Groups (Science, Impacts, and Mitigation).

Some months before the three Working Group reports received final approval, the IPCC prepared a brief "Summary for Policymakers" of each report. It is these three highly selective 15 to 20 page Summaries that largely inform the public policy debate over global warming.

IPCC officials claim and media subsequently report that the Assessment Reports and their Summaries represent the consensus views of the hundreds of scientists who have contributed to the reports. This claim is false. Each chapter of an Assessment Report is written by a team of authors, consisting of a coordinating lead author, lead authors, and many contributing authors. Contributors are each responsible for a small section, as short as one or two pages. Contributors are not asked by the IPCC whether they agree with anything else in the Assessment Report beyond their own small sections.

Teams of 15 to 25 people consisting of chapter lead authors and other IPCC officials prepare the Summaries for Policymakers. Their drafts are edited and then approved by representatives of the national governments that comprise the IPCC. As such, the Summaries reflect the political agenda of the proponents of global warming alarmism and often slant the content in that direction. Such reports are responsible for many of the myths about the science of global warming. The following . . . discusses some of the key myths promoted by the IPCC Summary for Policymakers of the Third Assessment Report's Working Group 1 as well as some other common myths.

Myth: The Last Century Was the Warmest in a Millennium

The Third Assessment Report's Working Group 1 Summary includes a graph that shows nearly stable global mean temperatures for the first 900 years of the past millennium and then a sharp increase in temperature during the 20th century. This "hockey stick" graph is the basis of the frequent claim that the last century was the warmest in the past thousand years.

This assertion is based on only one scientific article that compiled and analyzed only one set of tree rings out of the numerous paleo-climate data sets available. A wealth of research beginning with the father of modern climatology, Hubert H. Lamb, indicates that the Medieval Warm Period (from around 800 to 1200) was global and that global mean temperatures were higher than during the 20th century. The hockey stick also fails to show the Little Ice Age from around 1300 to 1850. Much research suggests that the Little Ice Age was the coldest period since the end of the last Ice Age 11,000 years ago. These errors in the hockey stick graph undermine the credibility of the claim that the 20th century was the warmest in the past millennium.

Myth: Global Warming Models Are Becoming More Accurate

Much of global warming theory is based on global warming computer models that have built-in assumptions about how various changes in the atmosphere could affect weather.

These models have consistently failed to adequately predict changes in climate because limited knowledge inhibits the scientific community's ability to account for all possible factors. Regarding these models, the Third Assessment's Summary claims that:

- "Confidence in the ability of models to project future climate has increased. Understanding of climate processes and their incorporation in climate models have improved, including water vapour, sea-ice dynamics, and ocean heat transport."

Yet Dr. Richard S. Lindzen, professor of meteorology at MIT [Massachusetts Institute of Technology] and a lead author of Chapter 7 of the TAR, commented on this claim:

- "This statement summarizes a chapter which points out that all these things are done poorly, and that no model comes close to realistically depicting clouds. Moreover, clouds and water vapor are so intimately related that it is inconceivable that one would get water vapor right and clouds wrong. It also ignores that it is the behavior of water vapor and clouds (the atmosphere's main greenhouse substances) that are responsible for model predictions of large warming. Increased CO_2 [carbon dioxide] alone, will produce little warming (about 1 degree Celsius for a doubling of CO_2). This point is made in Chapter 7."

Myth: Humans Are the Key Cause of Warming

The IPCC Summary observes that the global mean temperature increased by three-tenths of one degree Celsius in the second half of the 20th century, and then it claims: "There is new and stronger evidence that most of the warming observed over the last 50 years is attributed to human activities." This claim is contradicted by a report published in 2000 by the National Research Council (NRC) on *Reconciling Observations on Global Temperature Change*. The NRC's special committee concluded that surface temperature data showing a three-tenths of a degree Celsius rise in the global mean temperature since 1975 was accurate, but so too was the satellite temperature record compiled by scientists John Christy and Roy Spencer. Their satellite measurements show no significant increase in global

What Is the Greenhouse Effect?

The greenhouse effect should not be confused with anthropogenic (human-caused) global warming. Instead, the greenhouse effect is a natural process that keeps the Earth warm enough to sustain life. Certain gases in the atmosphere (conveniently called greenhouse gases) trap some incoming solar radiation, which in turn warms the earth's surface. Most of the heat trapped by the greenhouse effect is stored in the oceans rather than in the atmosphere.

The principal greenhouse gas is water vapor (which includes clouds). Water vapor constitutes more than 95 percent of total greenhouse gases. Trace greenhouse gases include carbon dioxide (CO_2), methane (CH_4), nitrous oxide (N_2O), hydrofluorocarbons (HFCs), perfluorocarbons (PFCs), and sulfur hexafluoride (SF_6). Water vapor is not included in the UN Framework Convention on Climate Change and Kyoto Protocol because the *direct* human impact on the amount of water vapor in the atmosphere is thought to be insignificant. All the trace greenhouse gases are covered by the Kyoto Protocol, but the principal focus is on reducing carbon dioxide emissions.

Carbon dioxide is a naturally-occurring, tasteless, odorless gas. Plants require carbon dioxide for photosynthesis. Animals produce CO_2 when they oxidize nutrients and exhale. At the beginning of the Industrial Revolution in the early 19th century, the Earth's atmosphere contained approximately 280 parts per million (ppm) of CO_2. As a result of burning hydrocarbons (coal, petroleum, and natural gas), CO_2 levels have risen to approximately 370 ppm today.

The pre-industrial CO_2 level of 280 ppm should not be taken as the normal or preferred level or the natural background level. CO_2 concentrations have fluctuated widely over geologic time. Recent research by Dr. Gregory J. Retallack indicates that CO_2 levels have fluctuated between 1,000 and 2,000 ppm over most of the past 300 million years and have only rarely declined to the current level.

Myron Ebell, *Environmental Source*, December 31, 2004.

---

mean temperature from 1979 to the present. Satellites measure temperatures in the lower troposphere. According to global warming theory, an increase in the greenhouse effect will first raise temperatures in the atmosphere, which will then warm the earth's surface. Therefore, the observed surface warming during the second half of the 20th century cannot plausibly be attributed to increasing greenhouse concentrations.

Myth: Global Temperatures Will Increase by 1.4 to 5.8 Degrees Celsius

According to the IPCC Summary, "The global average surface temperature is projected to increase by 1.4 to 5.8 degrees Celsius over the period 1990 to 2100. These results are for the full range of 35 SRES [Special Report Emission Scenario] scenarios, based on a number of climate models." The Second Assessment Report predicted temperature rises in the range of 1 to 3.5 degrees Celsius over the next 100 years. The Summary of the Third Assessment Report reaches a much higher prediction of 5.8 degrees Celsius (or 10.4 degrees Farenheit) by concocting a completely implausible scenario consisting of the assumptions that the whole world will raise its level of economic activity to that of the United States, will equal U.S. per capita energy consumption, and energy use will continue to be carbon intensive. Footnote 11 to the IPCC Summary adds: "This range does not include uncertainties in the modeling of radiative forcing, e.g. aerosol forcing uncertainties."

But the uncertainties regarding aerosol forcing are so large as to make the predictions entirely unreliable. The IPCC does not assign probabilities to the range of predicted temperature increases. A study conducted by researchers at the Joint Program on the Science and Policy of Global Change at MIT concluded that "there is far less than a 1 in 100 chance of a global mean surface temperature increase by 2100 as large as 5.8 degrees Celsius." They also concluded that "there is a 12 percent chance that the temperature change in 2100 would be less than the IPCC lower estimate." In other words, there is a 12 percent chance the climate change will be less than 1.4 degrees Celsius even using the highly questionable assumptions in the IPCC's computer models.

Myth: Sea Levels Will Rise Dramatically

Global warming doomsayers have long claimed that as the earth warms, the Antarctic and Greenland ice caps will melt, increasing sea levels. Some have predicted that the water will rise so high that coastal cities such as New York will soon become submerged in water.

Sea levels have been rising at varying rates since before the end of the last Ice Age 11,000 years ago—long before any manmade global warming is claimed to have begun. Sea levels will continue to rise until the next Ice Age begins as the Antarctic and Greenland Ice Sheets and glaciers continue to melt. Sea level rise over short periods is extremely difficult to determine, but it is believed that the rate of sea level rise has not increased over the past century when manmade global warming is claimed to have occurred. Future global warming may cause the rate of sea level rise to increase due to the thermal expansion of water and faster melting of the ice sheets.

Fortunately, if there is a sea level rise, we will be able to address associated problems. A report by the Pew Center on Climate Change, a booster group for energy suppression policies, estimated that the cost of rising sea levels for the United States would total $20 to $150 billion over the next 100 years. This is less than Americans currently spend on cat food per year ($4 billion). But more importantly, the estimated costs of mitigating a potential sea rise are hundreds of times less than estimated costs of global warming policies. The Kyoto Protocol cost estimates to the United States range from $225 to $400 billion annually, and the Protocol will do little to slow the rate of predicted global warming.

Myth: Global Warming Will Produce More Storms

Another warning is that global warming will cause more frequent or more intense severe weather events, such as hurricanes, droughts, and floods. There is no scientific basis to support this claim. Dr. William Gray, a Colorado State University scientist and one of the world's foremost hurricane experts, does not believe that global warming is affecting hurricanes: "It sure as hell ain't global warming," he bluntly noted on MSNBC.

That severe weather events are becoming more common is based on the rise of 24-hour television news cable channels and consequent increased television coverage of weather disasters. The claim that damages caused by hurricanes have increased is misleading. Insurance claims for hurricane damage have increased because the number and value of buildings in hurricane-prone areas such as Florida has increased dramatically. Moreover, insurance claims have not increased as a percentage of gross domestic product.

Myth: Global Warming Will Produce More Tropical Diseases

Global warming scaremongers also claim that climate changes will increase tropical diseases, bringing them into non-tropical areas. But the fact that such diseases are not common in the Western world now has nothing to do with climate. Instead, as Western nations grew wealthier, we developed measures to protect against the disease carrying insects and other vectors. Such measures include the use of tightly enclosed homes with screens and air conditioning (keeping bugs out) and vector control, including the use of pesticides.

In fact, before such measures were implemented, so-called "tropical diseases" such as malaria and dengue fever were common during the Little Ice Age in cities as far north as Washington, New York City, Toronto, London, and Stockholm. They were eradicated or controlled in these areas by public health measures and vector control. Major research by Dr. Paul Reiter of the U.S. Centers for Disease Control and Prevention concludes that potential global warming will not increase the frequency or range of these diseases. However, these diseases are still common in many poor tropical and sub-tropical countries because of the lack of adequate public health establishments, and because they lack the wealth that enables those in the Western world to avoid contact with disease-carrying organisms.

Myth: The Impacts of Global Warming Are All Negative

Global warming alarmism depends on the belief that the effects of human-caused climate change must be entirely bad. However, ecologists and economists are rapidly discovering that global warming could bring both beneficial and harmful effects. According to Yale University Professor Robert Mendelsohn, there has been a:

Near revolution that has occurred over the past decade in our understanding of the impacts of climate change. . . . The new research suggests that climate warming will not be as harmful as we once thought it might be. . . . The reduction in damage-estimates removes the urgency to engage in costly crash abatement programs. Our initial perspective on greenhouse gases suggested that we were rapidly approaching the edge of a cliff. Those fears now appear unfounded, for the impacts from climate warming seem to be relatively small for the next century. . . . These changes [in our understanding of climate change] are so dramatic that it is not clear whether the net economic effects from climate change over the next century will be harmful or helpful.

The most certain effect of rising carbon dioxide levels in the atmosphere is not global warming, but increased plant growth—leading to higher agricultural yields and more food to feed the world and greater biodiversity. Plants require carbon dioxide for photosynthesis. Most classes of plants developed when CO_2 levels were much higher than today. Hundreds of experiments conducted over the past half century have demonstrated increased plant growth with higher CO_2 levels. The pre-industrial CO_2 level is not necessarily the normal or preferred level.

> "High rates of population growth combined with high levels of consumption in rich countries are taking a heavy toll on the Earth's natural resources."

Environmental Problems Caused by Overpopulation Will Harm Humanity

Danielle Nierenberg and Mia MacDonald

As the world population continues to grow, food, water, and energy needs may not keep pace, argue Danielle Nierenberg and Mia MacDonald in the following viewpoint. Women in developing nations continue to have large numbers of children, which strains resources, the authors claim. Although the populations in developed countries grow more slowly, the people consume a greater proportion of the world's resources, the authors contend, so population in these nations is also a problem. To prevent hunger and environmental degradation, people must promote women's reproductive choices and encourage sustainable consumption practices worldwide, the authors claim. Nierenberg is a research associate and MacDonald is a policy analyst at the WorldWatch Institute, an environmental think tank.

As you read, consider the following questions:

1. What is the impact of new demographic trends, in Nierenberg and MacDonald's view?
2. In the authors' opinion, what have studies shown about women with more education?

Forty years ago, the world's women bore an average of six children each. Today, that number is just below three. In 1960, 10–15 percent of married couples in developing countries used a modern method of contraception; now, 60 percent do.

To a considerable extent, these simple facts sum up the change in the Earth's human population prospects, then and now. In the mid-1960s, it was not uncommon to think about the human population as a time bomb. In 1971, population biologist Paul Ehrlich estimated that if human numbers kept increasing at the high rates of the time, by around 2900 the planet would be teeming with sixty million billion people (that's 60,000,000,000,000,000). But the rate of population rise actually peaked in the 1960s and demographers expect a leveling-off of human numbers this century.

Every couple of years the United Nations [UN] Population Division issues projections of human population growth to 2050. In 2002, UN demographers predicted a somewhat different picture of human population growth to mid-century than what the "population bombers" thought likely a generation ago. World population, growing by 76 million people every year (about 240,000 people per day), will pass 6.4 billion [in 2004]. The latest UN mid-range estimate says there will be about 8.9 billion people on Earth by 2050. And, according to this new scenario, total population will begin to shrink over the next hundred years.

These numbers are leading some people to say that the population bomb has been defused. A few nations, such as Italy and Japan, are even worried that birth rates are too low and that their graying populations will be a drain on the economy. (Some studies suggest that China, the world's most populous country, may also "need" more people to help support the hundreds of millions who will retire in coming decades).

We're not out of the woods yet. While the annual rate of population growth has decreased since 1970—from about 2 percent to 1.3 percent today—*the rate is applied to a much larger population* than ever before, meaning that the added yearly increments to the population are also much larger. These numbers show that the largest generation in history has arrived: 1.2 billion people are between 10 and 19. In large measure, it will be their choices—those they have, and those they make—that determine where the global population meter rests by mid-century.

Population and Consumption

Potential for catastrophe persists. In many places, population growth is slowly smoldering but could turn into a fast burn. Countries as diverse as Ethiopia, the Democratic Republic of Congo, and Pakistan are poised to more than double their size by 2050 even as supplies of water, forests, and food crops are already showing signs of strain and other species are being squeezed into smaller and smaller ranges. Arid Yemen will likely see its population quadruple to 80 million by 2050. The UN estimates that populations in the world's 48 least-developed countries could triple by 2050. And if the world's women have, on average, a half a child more than the UN predicts, global population could grow to 10.6 billion by mid-century.

But it is a mistake to think that population growth is only a problem for developing countries. While consumption levels need to increase among the 2.8 billion people who now live on less than $2 a day, high rates of population growth combined with high levels of consumption in rich countries are taking a heavy toll on the Earth's natural resources:

- Carbon dioxide levels today are 18 percent higher than in 1960 and an estimated 31 percent higher than they were at the onset of the Industrial Revolution in 1750.
- Half the world's original forest cover is gone and another 30 percent is degraded or fragmented.
- Industrial fleets have fished out at least 90 percent of all large ocean predators—tuna, marlin, swordfish, cod, halibut, skate, and flounder—in just the past 50 years, according to a study in *Nature* in 2003.
- An estimated 10–20 percent of the world's cropland, and more than 70 percent of the world's rangelands, are degraded.

As global consumption of oil, meat, electricity, paper products, and a host of consumer goods rises, the impact of population numbers takes on a new relevance. Although each new person increases total demands on the Earth's resources, the size of each person's "ecological footprint"—the biologically productive area required to support that person—varies hugely from one to another. The largest eco-footprints belong to those in the industrialized world.

The Demographic Trends

Further, new demographic trends can have significant impacts as well. Since 1970, the number of people living together in one household has declined worldwide, as incomes have risen, urbanization has accelerated and families have gotten smaller. With fewer people sharing energy, appliances, and furnishings, consumption actually rises. A one-person household in the United States uses about 17 percent *more* energy per person than a two-person home.

And while some nations are getting nervous about declining birth rates, for most of the world the end of population growth is anything but imminent. Although fertility rates are ratcheting down, this trajectory is not guaranteed. Projections of slower population growth assume that more couples will be able to choose to have smaller families, and that investment in reproductive health keeps pace with rising demand. But along the route to the eventual leveling-off of global population, plateaus are possible. And smaller families are not guaranteed in countries where government resources are strained or where health care, education, and women's rights are low on the list of priorities.

In the West African country of Niger, for example, the availability of family planning and reproductive health services has declined, while birth rates have increased. According to a recent report by the World Bank, the average woman in Niger will give birth to eight children in her lifetime, up from seven in 1998 and more than women in any other nation. Niger is already bulging with young people; 50 percent of the population is under age 15 and 70 percent is under 25.

Biology Does Not Equal Destiny

A series of global conferences in the 1990s—spanning the Rio Earth Summit in 1992, the Cairo population conference

(1994), the Beijing women's conference (1995), and the UN's Millennium Summit in 2000—put issues of environment, development, poverty, and women's rights on the global policy table. As a result, discussions of the relationship between growing human numbers and the Earth's ability to provide are increasingly framed by the realities of gender relations. It is now generally agreed that while enabling larger numbers of women and men to use modern methods of family planning is essential, it is not sufficient. Expanding the choices, capacities, and agency of women has become a central thread in the population story. Consumption—what we need and what we want—is, too.

Many studies have shown that women with more education have smaller, healthier families, and that their children have a better chance of making it out of poverty. Likewise, wealthier women and those with the right to make decisions about their lives and bodies also have fewer children. And women who have the choice to delay marriage and child-bearing past their teens tend to have fewer children than those women—and there are millions of them still—who marry before they've completed the transition from adolescence. Equalizing relations between women and men is also a social good: not only is it just, but a recent World Bank report found that in developing countries where gender equality lags, efforts to combat poverty and increase economic growth lag, too.

Women's Reproductive Rights

Yet women's rights and voices remain suppressed or muted throughout the world. Over 100 million girls will be married before their 18th birthdays in the next decade, some as young as 8 or 9. Early childbearing is the leading cause of death and disability for women between the ages of 15 and 19 in developing countries. At least 350 million women still lack access to a full range of contraceptive methods, 10 years after the Cairo conference yielded a 20-year plan to balance the world's people with its resources. Demand for services will increase an estimated 40 per cent by 2025.

The assault of HIV/AIDS is also increasingly hurting women: more than 18 million women are living with HIV/AIDS, and in 2003 women's rate of infection for the first time equaled men's. In the region hardest hit, sub-Saharan Africa, 60 percent of adults living with HIV are women. Two-thirds of the world's 876 million illiterates are women and a majority of the 115 million children not attending grade school are girls. In no country in the world are women judged to have political, economic, and social power equal to that of men.

Even in the United States, women's reproductive rights are increasingly constrained by the growing number of restrictions and conditions on choice imposed by state and federal laws. Like the U.S. lifestyle, the [George W. Bush] Administration's blinkered view of sexuality has gone global. The United States has withheld $34 million from the UN Population Fund (UNFPA) every year of the Bush Administration due to a dispute over abortion. And the "global gag rule," a relic of the Reagan presidency reimposed by President [George W.] Bush, binds U.S. population assistance by making taboo any discussion of abortion in reproductive health clinics, even in countries where it is legal.

The impacts reach more deeply than the rhetoric: due to the loss of U.S. population funds, reproductive health services have been scaled back or eliminated in some of the world's poorest countries, precisely where fertility rates are highest and women's access to family planning most tenuous. In Kenya, for instance, the two main providers of reproductive health services refused to sign a pledge to enforce the gag rule, with the result that they lost funds and closed five family planning clinics, eliminating women's access to maternal health care, contraception, and voluntary counseling and testing for HIV/AIDS. In Ethiopia, where only 6 per cent of women use modern methods of contraception, the gag rule has cut a wide swath: clinics have reduced services, laid off staff and curtailed community health programs; many have suffered shortages of contraceptive supplies.

Meeting Women's Needs

A recent study by UNFPA and the Alan Guttmacher Institute estimated that meeting women's current unmet need for contraception would prevent each year:
- 23 million unplanned births
- 22 million induced abortions
- 1.4 million infant deaths
- 142,000 pregnancy related-deaths (including 53,000 from unsafe abortions); and
- 505,000 children losing their mothers due to pregnancy-related causes.

The non-medical benefits are not quantified but are considerable: greater self-esteem and decision-making power for women; higher productivity and income; increased health, nutrition, and education expenditures on each child; higher savings and investment rates; and increased equality between women and men. We know this from experience: recent research in the United States, for example, ascribes the large numbers of women entering law, medical, and other professional training programs in the 1970s to the expanded choices afforded by the wide availability of the Pill.

Despite these benefits, vast needs go unmet as the Cairo action plan remains underfunded. The United States is not the only culprit. UNFPA reports that donor funds for a basic package of reproductive health services and population data and policy work totaled about $3.1 billion in 2003— $2.6 billion less than the level agreed to in the ICPD [International Conference on Population and Development] Program. Developing country domestic resources were estimated at $11.7 billion, a major portion of which is spent by just a handful of large countries. A number of countries, particularly the poorest, rely heavily on donor funds to provide services for family planning, reproductive health, and HIV/AIDS, and to build data sets and craft needed policies.

[In 2005] donors will be expected to be contributing $6.1 billion annually, $3 billion more than what has already been spent. "A world that spends $800 billion to $1 trillion each year on the military can afford the equivalent of slightly more than one day's military spending to close Cairo's $3 billion external funding gap to save and improve the lives of millions of women and families in developing countries," says UNFPA's executive director, Thoraya Obaid. But as the world's priorities lie in other arenas, it is looking increasingly unlikely that the Cairo targets—despite their modest price tag in a world where the bill for a war can top $100 billion—will be met.

The Problem in Developed Nations

But it isn't only poor people in developing countries who will determine whether the more dire population scenarios pass from speculation to reality. Family size has declined in most wealthy nations, but the U.S. population grew by 32.7 million people (13.1 percent) during the 1990s, the largest number in any 10-year period in U.S. history. At about 280 million people, the United States is now the third most populous nation in the world and its population is expected to reach 400 million by 2050. A recent study suggests that if every person alive today consumed at the rate of an average person in the United States, three more planets would be required to fulfill these demands.

Whether or not birth rates continue to fall, consumption

levels and patterns (affluence), coupled with technology, take on new importance. The global consumer class—around 1.7 billion people, or more than a quarter of humanity—is growing rapidly. These people are collectively responsible for the vast majority of meat-eating, paper use, car driving, and energy consumption on the planet, as well as the resulting impact of these activities on its natural resources. As populations surge in developing countries and the world becomes increasingly globalized, more and more people have access to, and the means to acquire, a greater diversity of products and services than ever before.

It is the combined effect of human numbers and human consumption that creates such potent flash-points. Decisions about sexuality and lifestyle are among the most deeply personal and political decisions societies and their citizens can make. The fate of the human presence on the Earth will be shaped in large part by those decisions and how their implications unfold in the coming years. This population story's ending still hasn't been written.

"Humanity has . . . [made] the world safer and more comfortable for an ever larger portion of the world's population."

Overpopulation Does Not Threaten the Environment or Humanity

Ronald Bailey

Predictions that a growing population will inevitably lead to famine and environmental destruction are inaccurate, claims Ronald Bailey in the following viewpoint. In addition to tangible goods, he argues, humanity also produces ideas. The more people there are, the more ideas, he points out. These ideas engender new ways to produce more resources using less land and energy. According to Bailey, the best way to stave off environmental degradation and famine, then, is not to restrict population growth but to promote economic development, which leads to higher education levels and, in turn, more ideas. Bailey is an adjunct scholar with the Cato Institute, a libertarian think tank.

As you read, consider the following questions:

1. What two propositions did Thomas Malthus regard as self-evident, in Bailey's view?
2. Into what two types of productive inputs do New Growth Theorists divide the world, in Bailey's view?
3. What analogy about human society does the New Growth theory suggest, in the author's opinion?

Ronald Bailey, "The Law of Increasing Returns," *The National Interest*, Spring 2000. Copyright © 2000 by *The National Interest*. Reproduced by permission of the publisher and the author.

Two hundred years after Thomas Robert Malthus published *An Essay on the Principle of Population*, demographers, ecologists, economists, biologists and policymakers still debate his theory of population. Leading foundations spend scores of millions of dollars on population programs, while the United Nations holds international conferences on the topic and even has a specialized agency, the United Nations Population Fund, devoted to the issue. [In 1999] the Fund portentously declared that the world's population reached six billion on October 12 [1999]. Every year, hundreds of weighty studies and books pour from the universities and think tanks discussing what is to be done.

The Theory of Thomas Malthus

Malthus advanced two propositions that he regarded as completely self-evident. First, that "food is necessary for the existence of man", and second, that "the passion between the sexes is necessary and will remain nearly in its present state." Based on these propositions, Malthus famously concluded that "the power of population is indefinitely greater than the power in the earth to produce subsistence for man. Population, when unchecked, increases in a geometrical ratio. Subsistence increases only in an arithmetical ratio. A slight acquaintance with numbers will show the immensity of the first power in comparison with the second."

Malthus . . . further asserted that "population does invariably increase where there are the means of subsistence." Malthus' dismal summary of the situation in which humanity finds itself is that some portion of mankind must forever be starving to death; and, further, efforts to aid the starving will only lead to more misery, as those initially spared from famine bear too many children to feed with existing food supplies.

In his first edition of the *Essay*, Malthus argued that there were two "checks" on population, "preventive" and "positive." Preventive checks, those that prevent births, include abortion, infanticide and prostitution; positive checks include war, pestilence and famine. In later editions, he added a third check that he called "moral restraint", which includes voluntary celibacy, late marriage and the like. Moral restraint is basically just a milder version of the earlier preventive check. If all else fails to keep human numbers under control, Malthus chillingly concludes, "Famine seems to be the last, the most dreadful resource of nature. The power of population is so superior to the power in the earth to produce subsistence for man, that premature death must in some shape or other visit the human race. The vices of mankind are active and able ministers of depopulation. They are the precursors in the great army of destruction, and often finish the dreadful work themselves. But should they fail in this war of extermination, sickly seasons, epidemics, pestilence, and plague, advance in terrific array, and sweep off their thousands and ten thousands. Should success be still incomplete, gigantic inevitable famine stalks in the rear, and with one mighty blow, levels the population with the food of the world."

Applying the Principles

Malthus' principle of population has proved to be one of the most influential and contested theories in history. . . .

Naturalists, biologists and ecologists have since applied Malthusian theory not only to animals and plants, but to humans as well. Undeniably, his principle of population has an appealing simplicity, and has proved a fruitful hypothesis for ecology and population biology. It undergirds such biological concepts as carrying capacity, which is a measure of the population that a given ecosystem can support. The Kaibab Plateau deer, for example, is a famous case of an animal population outstripping its food supply. In the 1920s, the deer population expanded dramatically. In the absence of predators, a forage shortage ensued, which in turn led to a dramatic reduction of the deer population.

The Population Bomb

If the concept of carrying capacity can explain fluctuations in animal populations, some intellectuals have reasoned in the second half of the twentieth century, it should apply equally well to human populations. As Stanford University entomologist Paul Ehrlich has explained: "To ecologists who study animals, food and population often seem like sides of the same coin. If too many animals are devouring it, the food supply declines; too little food, the supply of animals declines. . . .

Homo sapiens is no exception to that rule, and at the moment it seems likely that food will be our limiting resource."

Overpopulation Is Not the Problem

Of course population can reach a point where, for a given level of technical know-how, and with a given social structure, more people means more environmental degradation and a lower standard of living for most. But there is no evidence that we are near such a population level. And there is no evidence that current poverty, hunger, and environmental degradation etc. owe their origins or tenacity in any significant degree to a population problem, but, instead, the evidence is abundant that these particular crimes against humanity are rooted in oppressive institutional structures and the abhorrent misallocations of labor and energy and maldistribution of product that they foster.

Michael Albert, *Z Magazine*, 2004.

In the late 1960s, Ehrlich was one of many biologists and agronomists who began to issue dire warnings about human "overpopulation", the most famous of which appeared in his book, *The Population Bomb* (1968). "The battle to feed all of humanity is over", Ehrlich wrote. "In the 1970s, the world will undergo famines—hundreds of millions of people are going to starve to death in spite of any crash programs embarked on now." Later, in an article for the first Earth Day in 1970, Ehrlich outlined a horrific scenario in which 65 million Americans and 4 billion other people would die of starvation in a "Great Die-Off" between 1980 and 1989. And in 1990 Ehrlich and his wife Anne published *The Population Explosion*, where they once again asserted that, "One thing seems safe to predict: starvation and epidemic disease will raise the death rates over most of the planet." In these gloomy forecasts, Ehrlich was far from alone. In 1967, William and Paul Paddock asserted in their book, *Famine 1975!*, that, "The famines which are now approaching . . . are for a surety, inevitable. . . . In fifteen years the famines will be catastrophic." Today, the Worldwatch Institute, a Washington, DC, environmentalist advocacy group chaired by Lester Brown, still has a solid Malthusian focus.

Food is not the only resource said to be in short supply. In

1972 the Club of Rome, a group of politicians, businessmen and senior international bureaucrats, famously commissioned The Limits to Growth report, which concluded: "If the present growth trends in world population, industrialization, pollution, food production, and resource depletion continue unchanged, the limits to growth on this planet will be reached sometime in the next one hundred years. The probable result will be a rather sudden and uncontrollable decline in both population and industrial capacity."

This is Malthus writ large: not only will humanity run out of food, but it will also run out of non-renewable resources like minerals and fossil fuels. . . .

Theories of Economic Growth

For decades, economists essentially used a two-factor model in which economic growth was accounted for by adding more labor and more capital to create more goods. The problem with this model is that over time growth must halt when the marginal value of the goods produced equals the cost of the labor and capital used to produce them. This neoclassical model of economic growth was elaborated in the 1950s by Nobelist Robert Solow and his colleagues, and was later incorporated into The Limits to Growth computer model. Relying on it, MIT [Massachusetts Institute of Technology] researchers predicted eventual collapse as the inevitable result of continued economic and population growth.

In the last two decades, economic forecasters, following the lead of economist Paul Romer, have made a conceptual breakthrough that has enabled them to describe more rigorously and accurately—and differently—how economic growth occurs and how, with the proper social institutions, it can continue for the foreseeable future. Romer explains this approach, which has come to be known as the New Growth Theory:

> New growth theorists now start by dividing the world into two fundamentally different types of productive inputs that can be called "ideas" and "things." Ideas are nonrival goods that could be stored in a bit string. Things are rival goods with mass (or energy). With ideas and things, one can explain how economic growth works. Nonrival ideas can be used to rearrange things, for example, when one follows a

recipe and transforms noxious olives into tasty and healthful olive oil. Economic growth arises from the discovery of new recipes and the transformation of things from low to high value configurations.

Decoding the clunky economic terminology, "rival" goods are simply things that cannot be used by two or more persons at once, e.g., cars, drill presses, computers, even human bodies and brains. "Nonrival" goods can be used by any number of people simultaneously, e.g., recipes for bread, blueprints for houses, techniques for growing corn, formulas for pharmaceuticals, scientific principles like the law of gravity, and computer programs.

To understand the potency of ideas, consider that a few decades ago silicon was used primarily to make glass. Today it is a crucial component in microchips and optical fibers. Again, until fairly recently petroleum was known mainly as a nuisance for people engaged in drilling water wells; its use as a cheap lighting replacement for increasingly scarce whale oil only began in the 1890s, and soon after came the internal combustion engine.

We make ourselves better off, then, not by increasing the amount of resources on planet earth—that is, of course, fixed—but by rearranging resources we already have available so that they provide us with more of what we want. This process of improvement has been going on ever since the first members of our species walked the earth. We have moved from heavy earthenware pots to ultrathin plastics and lightweight aluminum cans. To cook our food we have shifted from wood-intensive campfires to clean, efficient natural gas. By using constantly improving recipes, humanity has avoided the Malthusian trap while at the same time making the world safer and more comfortable for an ever larger portion of the world's population. . . .

Reframing the Problems

Insights from New Growth Theory reframe many environmental problems and suggest some surprising solutions. For example, one of the global environmental problems most commonly attributed to population and economic growth is the loss of tropical forests. But is growth really to blame? According to the Consultative Group on International Agricultural Research, the chief factor that drives deforestation in developing countries is not commercial logging but "poor farmers who have no other option to feeding their families other than slashing and burning a patch of forest. . . . Slash-and-burn agriculture results in the loss or degradation of some 25 million acres of land per year."

By contrast, the United States today farms less than half of the land that it did in the 1920s but produces far more food now than it did then. The key, of course, is technology. In fact, available farming technology from developed countries could prevent, and in many cases reverse, the loss of tropical forests and other wildlife habitat around the globe. Unfortunately, institutional barriers, the absence of secure property rights, corrupt governments and a lack of education prevent its widespread diffusion and, hence, environmental restoration.

Pollution Declined with Population Growth

Another environmental problem frequently attributed to population growth is pollution. In 1972 The Limits to Growth computer model projected that pollution would skyrocket as population increased: "Virtually every pollutant that has been measured as a function of time appears to be increasing exponentially." But once again, the new Malthusians had things exactly backward. Since 1972, America's population has risen 26 percent and its economy has more than doubled. Western Europe and Japan have experienced similar rates of growth. Yet, instead of increasing as predicted, air pollutants have dramatically declined.

In fact, a growing body of literature suggests that in most cases there are thresholds of wealth at which the amount of a pollutant begins to decline. Department of Interior analyst Indur Goklany calls these thresholds the "environmental transition." What this means is that when people rise above mere subsistence, they begin demanding amenities such as clean air and water. The first environmental transition is clean drinking water. Goklany has found that the level of fecal coliform bacteria in rivers, which is a good measure of water pollution, peaks when average per capita incomes reach $1,400 per year. The next transition occurs when particulates like smoke and soot peak at $3,200. And again, levels of sulfur dioxide peak at about $3,700.

Targeting Rich Nations

Not surprisingly, committed Malthusians reject such findings. Paul Ehrlich, for instance, stubbornly insists that, "Most people do not recognize that, at least in rich nations, economic growth is the *disease*, not the cure." [emphasis in original] To counteract the "disease" of economic growth, Maurice King recommends that people in the "privileged North" should engage in "the deliberate quest of poverty" to curb their "luxurious resource consumption."

The favored target of such critiques is the United States, whose citizens are supposedly consuming more than their fair share of the world's goods and causing more than their fair share of its ills. The average American, however, is not only a consumer but a producer of both goods and ideas. Americans and Europeans get more done with relatively less because of their higher levels of education, greater access to productive tools, superior infrastructure, democratic governments and free markets. As a consequence, output per hour of labor in the United States today is ten times what it was a hundred years ago. Thus, the average Westerner creates far more resources, especially knowledge and technology, than she or he consumes. Thus, too, both Western economies and environments are improving simultaneously.

The Benefits of Growth

All that said, if the right social institutions are lacking—democratic governance, secure private property, free markets—it is possible for a nation to fall into the Malthusian trap of rising poverty and increasing environmental degradation. The economies of many countries in Africa are declining, not because of high population growth rates or lack of resources, but because they have failed to implement the basic policies for encouraging economic growth: namely, widespread education, secure property rights and democratic governance.

Democratic governance and open markets have in fact

proved indispensable for the prevention of famine in modern times. Nobel Prize-winning economist Amartya Sen notes that "in the terrible history of famines in the world, there is hardly any case in which a famine has occurred in a country that is independent and democratic, with an uncensored press." Why is this? Because, says Sen, "so long as famines are relatively costless for the government, with no threat to its survival or credibility, effective actions to prevent famines do not have the urgency to make them inescapable imperatives for the government." Along with Romer and other theorists, Sen also argues that general economic growth, not just growth in food output, is crucial to ending the threat of famine in Africa. He calls "for measures to encourage and enhance technical change, skill formation and productivity—both in agriculture and in other fields."

Contemporary Malthusians liken humanity to a car travelling one hundred miles per hour on a foggy road. And they warn of dire consequences if we do not slow down. But if we adopt institutions and regulations that slow the pace of innovation, we may find ourselves depleting our current energy supplies before they can be replaced by new ones. New Growth Theory suggests that a better analogy might be that human society is an airplane cloaked in clouds flying at a speed of six hundred miles per hour. If the plane slows down, it will lose air speed and may crash before arriving safely at its destination.

We cannot deplete the supply of ideas, designs and recipes. They are immaterial and limitless, and therefore not bound in any meaningful sense by the second law of thermodynamics. Surely no one believes that humanity has already devised all of the methods to conserve, locate and exploit new sources of energy, or that the flow of ideas to improve houses, transportation, communications, medicine and farming has suddenly dried up. Though far too many of our fellow human beings are caught in local versions of the Malthusian trap, we must not mistake the situation of that segment as representing the future of all of humanity and the earth itself; it is, instead, a dwindling remnant of an unhappy past. Misery is not the inevitable lot of humanity, nor is the ruin of the natural world a foregone conclusion.

Periodical Bibliography

The following articles have been selected to supplement the diverse views presented in this chapter.

Hussein A. Amery   "Water Wars in the Middle East: A Looming Threat," *Geographical Journal*, December 2002.

Edward B. Barbier   "Water and Economic Growth," *Economic Record*, March 2004.

Andrew Brackenbury   "Global Population," *Geographical*, March 2005.

Kathryn Brown   "Water Scarcity: Forecasting the Future with Spotty Data. While Global Water Models Warn of Parched Days Ahead, Scientists Worry That Another Pressing Scarcity Is Information," *Science*, August 9, 2002.

Christianity Today   "Heat Stroke: The Climate for Addressing Global Warming Is Improving," October 2004.

Clifton Coles   "The Growing Water Crisis: Given the Growing Scarcity of Water, It's Time to Change Water Policies Worldwide," *Futurist*, September/October 2003.

Clive Crook   "The State of the World: Richer, Cleaner, Better," *National Journal*, January 1, 2000.

Economist   "A Canary in the Coal Mine: Climate Change," November 13, 2004.

Economist   "Hotting Up: Climate Change and Politics," February 5, 2005.

Angela Eiss et al.   "Self-Destruct," *New Scientist*, April 28, 2001.

Steven F. Hayward   "Cooled Down: The Global-Warming Hype Is Running Out of (Greenhouse?) Gas, as It Very Much Deserves," *National Review*, January 31, 2005.

Margaret M. Jobe   "The State of World Population 2000: Lives Together, Worlds Apart; Men and Women in a Time of Change," *Library Journal*, May 15, 2001.

D. Gale Johnson   "On Population and Resources: A Comment," *Population and Development Review*, December 2001.

Nels Johnson, Carmen Revenga, and Jaime Echeverria   "Managing Water for People and Nature," *Science*, May 11, 2001.

Chris Mooney   "A Call for Attention to Climate Change," *Skeptical Inquirer*, November/December 2004.

J. Madeleine Nash   "Where the Waters Are Rising," *Time*, April 25, 2005.

Janet L. Sawin   "Water Scarcity Could Overwhelm the Next Generation," *World Watch*, July/August 2003.

Noelle Eckley Selin   "Mercury Rising: Is Global Action Needed to Protect Human Health and the Environment?" *Environment*, January/February 2005.

Jeanne Winner   "The Social Relations of Health and Disease," *Dollars & Sense*, May 2001.

CHAPTER 4

What Will Be the Future of the Global Community?

Chapter Preface

Many experts and laypeople alike are troubled by the impact terrorism might have on humanity's future. One of many controversies in the debate over the future of the global community is whether globalization will foster or reduce terrorism. While some analysts see globalization as an effective way to eliminate what they claim are the core causes of terrorism—poverty and political repression—others believe that globalization exacerbates these conditions and thus cultivates terrorists.

For some commentators, globalization is an effective weapon against terrorism because it promotes prosperity and freedom and will thus improve the future of the global community. These analysts argue that the people of nations closed to globalization often live in poverty and are politically repressed, conditions that contribute to extremism. Free-market scholar Brink Lindsey maintains, for example, that the conditions in some Muslim nations foster terrorism. "The Muslim world's woeful deficits in economic and political freedom surely deserve much of the blame" for the rise of terrorism, claims Lindsey. "Widespread poverty, high unemployment, the absence of opportunities for upward mobility, brutal and corrupt ruling elites, the stifling of dissent, the exasperation caused by seeing spectacular success elsewhere in the world—all stoke the rage and despair that win new converts to Islamist extremism," he asserts. It follows, Lindsey reasons, that promoting globalization in the Muslim world will impede the growth of terrorism. According to Lindsey, "The hope is that better integration of Arab countries into the global economy will initiate a virtuous circle of increased growth and broader economic reforms, and that, in turn, a freer and more prosperous Middle East will be less susceptible to the radical Islamist movements that support and perpetrate terrorism."

However, according to critics, globalization does not promote prosperity and freedom. In fact, they argue, it cultivates the economic insecurity and exclusion that breeds terrorists and thus poses a threat to the future of the global community. What globalization supporters call economic openness—

trade with multinational corporations—often destroys small-scale industry and farming, these analysts claim. According to activist Vandana Shiva, in India, her native country, economic "openness" for a multinational corporation means economic "closure" for local producers. For example, an open market for a large agribusiness, she asserts, means the closure of local farms that can't compete. This closure—the destruction of jobs and livelihoods—creates the economic insecurity and frustration that can lead to terrorism, Shiva claims. "As resources are snatched by global corporations, as livelihoods and jobs are destroyed to transform our economies into markets for products from [multinational corporations], economic insecurity is created. This insecurity becomes fertile ground for fundamentalism, hatred, fear and intolerance," Shiva argues. "Economic insecurity," she contends "creates inflammable societies that become vulnerable to terrorism and fundamentalism. Terrorism is a child of exclusion and insecurity. Both are unavoidable outcomes of globalization."

Whether globalization fosters or combats terrorism remains controversial. The authors in the following chapter share their views on other questions concerning the future of the global community.

"Average incomes have indeed been growing, but so has the income gap between rich and poor countries."

The Gap Between Rich and Poor Nations Is Growing

Bruce R. Scott

According to Harvard University business professor Bruce R. Scott in the following viewpoint, the income gap between rich and poor countries is growing. Theoretically, free trade should increase income worldwide and ultimately reduce the income gap, Scott maintains. In reality, he claims, free trade is not truly free since rich nations can impose immigration and agricultural barriers that advance their own economic interests at the expense of poor nations. For example, Scott asserts, since agriculture is often the primary export of poor countries, barriers erected by rich nations that prohibit agricultural imports keep poor nations poor.

As you read, consider the following questions:

1. In Scott's opinion, why have economists and policy makers failed to realize that free markets do not benefit all nations?
2. In addition to the freeing of prices, what does economic development require, in the author's view?
3. What kind of "catch-up" models does the author suggest no longer work?

Bruce R. Scott, "The Great Divide in the Global Village," *Foreign Affairs*, vol. 80, January/February 2001. Copyright © 2001 by the Council on Foreign Relations, Inc. All rights reserved. Reproduced by permission of the publisher, www.foreign affairs.org.

M ainstream economic thought promises that globalization will lead to a widespread improvement in average
incomes. Firms will reap increased economies of scale in a
larger market, and incomes will converge as poor countries
grow more rapidly than rich ones. In this "win-win" perspective, the importance of nation-states fades as the "global village" grows and market integration and prosperity take hold.

Incomes Are Diverging

But the evidence paints a different picture. Average incomes
have indeed been growing, but so has the income gap between rich and poor countries. Both trends have been evi-
dent for more than 200 years, but improved global communications have led to an increased awareness among the poor
of income inequalities and heightened the pressure to emi-
grate to richer countries. In response, the industrialized nations have erected higher barriers against immigration, making the world economy seem more like a gated community
than a global village. And although international markets for
goods and capital have opened up since World War II and
multilateral organizations now articulate rules and monitor
the world economy, economic inequality among countries
continues to increase. Some two billion people earn less than
$2 per day.

At first glance, there are two causes of this divergence between economic theory and reality. First, the rich countries
insist on barriers to immigration and agricultural imports.
Second, most poor nations have been unable to attract much
foreign capital due to their own government failings. These
two issues are fundamentally linked: by forcing poor people
to remain in badly governed states, immigration barriers
deny those most in need the opportunity to "move up" by
"moving out." In turn, that immobility eliminates a potential source of pressure on ineffective governments, thus facil-
itating their survival.

Since the rich countries are unlikely to lower their agricultural and immigration barriers significantly, they must
recognize that politics is a key cause of economic inequality.
And since most developing countries receive little foreign
investment, the wealthy nations must also acknowledge that

the "Washington consensus," which assumes that free markets will bring about economic convergence, is mistaken. If they at least admit these realities, they will abandon the notion that their own particular strategies are the best for all countries. In turn, they should allow poorer countries considerable freedom to tailor development strategies to their own circumstances. In this more pragmatic view, the role of the state becomes pivotal.

A Self-Serving World-View

Why have economists and policymakers not come to these conclusions sooner? Since the barriers erected by rich countries are seen as vital to political stability, leaders of those countries find it convenient to overlook them and focus instead on the part of the global economy that has been liberalized. The rich countries' political power in multilateral organizations makes it difficult for developing nations to challenge this self-serving world-view. And standard academic solutions may do as much harm as good, given their focus on economic stability and growth rather than on the institutions that underpin markets. Economic theory has ignored the political issues at stake in modernizing institutions, incorrectly assuming that market-based prices can allocate resources appropriately.

The fiasco of reform in Russia has forced a belated reappraisal of this blind trust in markets. Many observers now admit that the transition economies needed appropriate property rights and an effective state to enforce those rights as much as they needed the liberalization of prices. Indeed, liberalization without property rights turned out to be the path to gangsterism, not capitalism. China, with a more effective state, achieved much greater success in its transition than did Russia, even though Beijing proceeded much more slowly with liberalization and privatization.

Economic development requires the transformation of institutions as well as the freeing of prices, which in turn requires political and social modernization as well as economic reform. The state plays a key role in this process; without it, developmental strategies have little hope of succeeding. The creation of effective states in the developing world will not

Widening Income Gap Between Regions
Gross domestic product per capita

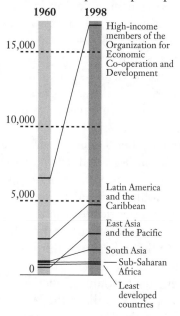

| 1960 | 1998 |

15,000 — High-income members of the Organization for Economic Co-operation and Development

10,000

5,000 — Latin America and the Caribbean

East Asia and the Pacific

South Asia

0 — Sub-Saharan Africa

Least developed countries

United Nations, *Human Development Report*, 2001.

be driven by familiar market forces, even if pressures from capital markets can force fiscal and monetary discipline. And in a world still governed by "states rights," real progress in achieving accountable governments will require reforms beyond the mandates of multilateral institutions.

Going with the Flow

In theory, globalization provides an opportunity to raise incomes through increased specialization and trade. This opportunity is conditioned by the size of the markets in question, which in turn depends on geography, transportation costs, communication networks, and the institutions that underpin markets. Free trade increases both the size of the market and the pressure to improve economic performance. Those who are most competitive take advantage of the enhanced market opportunities to survive and prosper.

Neoclassical economic theory predicts that poor countries should grow faster than rich ones in a free global market. Capital from rich nations in search of cheaper labor should flow to poorer economies, and labor should migrate from low-income areas toward those with higher wages. As a result, labor and capital costs—and eventually income—in rich and poor areas should eventually converge.

The U.S. economy demonstrates how this theory can work in a free market with the appropriate institutions. Since the 1880s, a remarkable convergence of incomes among the country's regions has occurred. The European Union has witnessed a similar phenomenon, with the exceptions of Greece and Italy's southern half, the Mezzogiorno. What is important, however, is that both America and the EU enjoy labor and capital mobility as well as free internal trade.

But the rest of the world does not fit this pattern. The most recent World Development Report shows that real per capita incomes for the richest one-third of countries rose by an annual 1.9 percent between 1970 and 1995, whereas the middle third went up by only 0.7 percent and the bottom third showed no increase at all. In the Western industrial nations and Japan alone, average real incomes have been rising about 2.5 percent annually since 1950—a fact that further accentuates the divergence of global income. These rich countries account for about 60 percent of world GDP [gross domestic product] but only 15 percent of world population.

Excluding Labor

Why is it that the poor countries continue to fall further behind? One key reason is that most rich countries have largely excluded the international flow of labor into their markets since the interwar period. As a result, low-skilled labor is not free to flow across international boundaries in search of more lucrative jobs. From an American or European perspective, immigration appears to have risen in recent years, even approaching its previous peak of a century ago in the United States. Although true, this comparison misses the central point. Billions of poor people could improve their standard of living by migrating to rich countries. But in 1997, the United States allowed in only 737,000 immigrants from developing nations, while Europe admitted about 665,000. Taken together, these flows are only 0.04 percent of all potential immigrants.

The point is not that the rich countries should permit unfettered immigration. A huge influx of cheap labor would no doubt be politically explosive; many European countries have already curtailed immigration from poor countries for fear of a severe backlash. But the more salient issue is that rich nations who laud liberalism and free markets are rejecting those very principles when they restrict freedom of movement. The same goes for agricultural imports. Both Europe and Japan have high trade barriers in agriculture, while the United States remains modestly protectionist.

Mainstream economic theory does provide a partial rationalization for rich-country protectionism: Immigration barriers need not be a major handicap to poor nations because they can be offset by capital flows from industrialized economies to developing ones. In other words, poor people need not demand space in rich countries because the rich will send their capital to help develop the poor countries. This was indeed the case before World War I, but it has not been so since World War II.

The Impact of Direct Investment

But the question of direct investment, which typically brings technologies and know-how as well as financial capital, is more complicated than theories would predict. The total stock of foreign direct investment did rise almost sevenfold from 1980 to 1997, increasing from 4 percent to 12 percent of world GDP during that period. But very little has gone to the poorest countries. In 1997, about 70 percent went from one rich country to another, 8 developing countries received about 20 percent, and the remainder was divided among more than 100 poor nations. According to the World Bank, the truly poor countries received less than 7 percent of the foreign direct investment to all developing countries in 1992–98. At the same time, the unrestricted opening of capital markets in developing countries gives larger firms from rich countries the opportunity for takeovers that are reminiscent of colonialism. It is not accidental that rich countries insist on open markets where they have an advantage and barriers in agriculture and immigration, where they would be at a disadvantage.

As for the Asian "tigers" [Taiwan, Hong Kong, South Korea and Singapore], their strong growth is due largely to their high savings rate, not foreign capital. Singapore stands out because it has enjoyed a great deal of foreign investment, but it has also achieved one of the highest domestic-savings rates in the world, and its government has been a leading influence on the use of these funds. China is now repeating this pattern, with a savings rate of almost 40 percent of GDP. This factor, along with domestic credit creation, has been its key motor of economic growth. China now holds more than $100 billion in low-yielding foreign-exchange reserves, the second largest reserves in the world.

In short, global markets offer opportunities for all, but opportunities do not guarantee results. Most poor countries have been unable to avail themselves of much foreign capital or to take advantage of increased market access. True, these countries have raised their trade ratios (exports plus imports) from about 35 percent of their GDP in 1981 to almost 50 percent in 1997. But without the Asian tigers, developing-country exports remain less than 25 percent of world exports.

Part of the problem is that the traditional advantages of poor countries have been in primary commodities (agriculture and minerals), and these categories have shrunk from about 70 percent of world trade in 1900 to about 20 percent at the end of the century. Opportunities for growth in the world market have shifted from raw or semiprocessed commodities toward manufactured goods and services—and, within these categories, toward more knowledge-intensive segments. This trend obviously favors rich countries over poor ones, since most of the latter are still peripheral players in the knowledge economy. (Again, the Asian tigers are the exception. In 1995, they exported as much in high-technology goods as did France, Germany, Italy, and Britain combined—which together have three times the population of the tigers.) . . .

Playing Catch-Up

Globalization offers opportunities for all nations, but most developing countries are very poorly positioned to capitalize on them. Malarial climates, limited access to navigable water, long distances to major markets, and unchecked population growth are only part of the problem. Such countries also have very unequal income structures inherited from colonial regimes, and these patterns of income distribution are hard to change unless prompted by a major upheaval such as a war or a revolution. But as serious as these disadvantages are, the greatest disadvantage has been the poor quality of government.

If today's global opportunities are far greater and potentially more accessible than at any other time in world history, developing countries are also further behind than ever before. Realistic political logic suggests that weak governments need to show that they can manage their affairs much better before they pretend to have strategic ambitions. So what kind of catch-up models could they adopt?

Substituting domestic goods for imports was the most popular route to economic development prior to the 1980s. But its inward orientation made those who adopted it unable to take advantage of the new global opportunities and ultimately it led to a dead end. Although the United States enjoyed success with such a strategy from 1790 until 1940, no developing country has a home market large enough to support a modern economy today. The other successful early growth model was European mercantilism, namely export promotion, as pioneered by Venice, the Dutch republic, Britain, and Germany. Almost all of the East Asian success stories, China included, are modern versions of the export-oriented form of mercantilism.

Problems of Shareholder Capitalism

For its part, free trade remains the right model for rich countries because it provides decentralized initiatives to search for tomorrow's market opportunities. But it does not necessarily promote development. Britain did not adopt free trade until the 1840s, long after it had become the world's leading industrial power. The prescription of lower trade barriers may help avoid even worse strategies at the hands of bad governments, but the Washington-consensus model remains best suited for those who are ahead rather than behind.

Today's shareholder capitalism brings additional threats to poor countries, first by elevating compensation for successful executives, and second by subordinating all activities to those that maximize shareholder value. Since 1970, the estimated earnings of an American chief executive have gone from 30 times to 450 times that of the average worker. In the leading developing countries, this ratio is still less than 50. Applying a similar "market-friendly" rise in executive compensation within the developing world would therefore only aggravate the income gap, providing new ammunition for populist politicians. In addition, shareholder capitalism calls for narrowing the managerial focus to the interests of shareholders, even if this means dropping activities that offset local market imperfections. A leading South African bank has shed almost a million small accounts—mostly held by blacks—to raise its earnings per share. Should this bank, like its American counterparts, have an obligation to serve its community, including its black members, in return for its banking license?

Poor nations must improve the effectiveness of their institutions and bureaucracies in spite of entrenched opposition and poorly paid civil servants. As the journalist Thomas Friedman has pointed out, it is true that foreign-exchange traders can dump the currencies of poorly managed countries, thereby helping discipline governments to restrain their fiscal deficits and lax monetary policies. But currency pressures will not influence the feudal systems in Pakistan and Saudi Arabia, the theocracies in Afghanistan and Iran, or the kleptocracies in Kenya or southern Mexico. The forces of capital markets will not restrain Brazilian squatters as they take possession of "public lands" or the slums of Rio de Janeiro or Sao Paulo, nor will they help discipline landlords and vigilantes in India's Bihar as they fight for control of their state. Only strong, accountable government can do that.

Looking Ahead

Increased trade and investment have indeed brought great improvements in some countries, but the global economy is hardly a win-win situation. Roughly one billion people earn less than $1 per day, and their numbers are growing. Economic resources to ameliorate such problems exist, but the political and administrative will to realize the potential of these resources in poor areas is lacking. Developing-nation governments need both the pressure to reform their administrations and institutions, and the access to help in doing so. But sovereignty removes much of the external pressure, while immigration barriers reduce key internal motivation. And the Washington consensus on the universality of the rich-country model is both simplistic and self-serving.

The world needs a more pragmatic, country-by-country approach, with room for neomercantilist regimes until such countries are firmly on the convergence track. Poor nations should be allowed to do what today's rich countries did to get ahead, not be forced to adopt the laissez-faire approach. Insisting on the merits of comparative advantage in low-wage, low-growth industries is a sure way to stay poor. And continued poverty will lead to rising levels of illegal immigration and low-level violence, such as kidnappings and vigilante justice, as the poor take the only options that remain. Over time, the rich countries will be forced to pay more attention to the fortunes of the poor—if only to enjoy their own prosperity and safety.

*"The well-being of the vast majority of
the world's population has improved and
continues to improve."*

Human Well-Being Is
Increasing Throughout
the World

Indur M. Goklany

The well-being of most of the world's people continues to
improve, maintains Indur M. Goklany in the following viewpoint. The real measure of humanity's progress, he argues, is
not income but well-being. The fact that more people
worldwide are free from hunger despite dire predictions of
famine reflects progress, he asserts. Moreover, infant mortality has decreased, and life expectancy has increased across
the globe, Goklany claims. He concludes that while income
may be increasing more slowly in some nations than in others, most of humanity is experiencing the benefits of economic and technological globalization. Goklany is an independent scholar with several libertarian think tanks.

As you read, consider the following questions:
1. According to Goklany, why has the real price of food
   never been lower?
2. In the author's opinion, in what regions has infant
   mortality improved the least?
3. What two reasons does Goklany give for the drop in life
   expectancy in sub-Saharan Africa?

Indur M. Goklany, "The Globalization of Human Well-Being," *Policy Analysis*,
August 22, 2002. Copyright © 2002 by the Cato Institute. All rights reserved.
Reproduced by permission.

M uch of the debate over globalization and its merits has revolved around the issues of income inequality and whether in the past few decades globalization has made the rich richer and the poor poorer. For example, Laura D'Andrea Tyson, former national economic adviser in the [Bill] Clinton administration, and others claimed that "as globalization has intensified, the gap between per capita incomes in rich and poor countries has widened." David Dollar and Aart Kraay, economists at the World Bank, have challenged such statements, countering that "the best evidence available shows the exact opposite to be true . . . [and that] . . . the current wave of globalization, which started around 1980, has actually promoted economic equality and reduced poverty." Regardless of where the truth may lie, these arguments miss the point. The central issue with respect to globalization is neither income inequality nor whether it is getting larger; rather it is whether globalization advances human well-being and, if inequalities in well-being have indeed expanded, whether that is because the rich have advanced at the expense of the poor.

But as opponents of globalization frequently note, human well-being is not synonymous with wealth, nor—to echo a catchy anti-globalization slogan—can you eat GDP [gross domestic product]. To conflate the two is to confuse ends with means. While wealth or per capita income (as measured by gross domestic product per capita) is probably the best indicator of material well-being, its greater importance stems from the fact that it either helps provide societies (and individuals) the means to improve other, probably more important, measures of human well-being (such as freedom from hunger, health, mortality rates, child labor, educational levels, access to safe water and sanitation, and life expectancy) or is associated with other desirable indicators (such as adherence to the rule of law, government transparency, economic freedom, and, to some extent, political freedom). In fact, . . . analyses of cross-country data show that although these other indicators generally improve as per capita income rises, their relationships are not linear. The improvements are usually rapid at low levels of economic development but slow down or, in some cases, halt altogether as they reach their practical or rhetorical limits. Therefore, per capita income would not, by itself, be a good measure of human well-being, and any determination of whether globalization has benefited humanity in general, or favors the rich at the expense of the poor, should be based on an examination of how these more relevant measures of human well-being have evolved as globalization has advanced. . . .

Hunger and Undernourishment

Concerns about the world's ability to feed its burgeoning population have been around at least since [Thomas] Malthus's *Essay on Population*, published 200 years ago. Initially the concern was global. But by the 1950s and 1960s, despite the privations of the Great Depression and World War II, it seemed that the problem, if any, would be restricted to developing countries. Several neo-Malthusians, such as Paul Ehrlich, author of *Population Bomb*, and [William and Paul] Paddock, confidently predicted apocalyptic famines in the latter part of the 20th century in the developing world. But remarkably, despite an unprecedented increase in the demand for food fueled by equally unprecedented population and economic growth, the average inhabitant has never been better fed and less likely to be hungry and undernourished.

Between 1950 and 2000, world population increased by 140 percent and per capita income by more than 170 percent. Yet, because of the enormous increase in agricultural productivity and trade, the real price of food has never been lower. Low food prices ensure that the benefits of increased production are distributed broadly and food surpluses flow voluntarily to deficit areas. As a result, worldwide food supplies per capita have improved steadily during the past half century. Between 1961 and 1999, the average daily food supplies per person increased 24 percent globally, from 2,257 calories to 2,808 calories. The increase was even more rapid in developing countries where it increased 39 percent, from 1,932 to 2,684 calories.

The improvements for Indians and Chinese—40 percent of humanity—are especially remarkable. By 1999, China's average daily food supplies had gone up 82 percent to 3,044 calories from a barely subsistence level of 1,636 calories in

1961 (a famine year). India's went up 48 percent to 2,417 calories from 1,635 calories in 1950–51.

Why Hunger Still Persists

However, . . . improvements in per capita food supplies have been slower where for whatever reason—war, political instability, or failed policies and institutions—economic development has lagged. For instance, between 1961 and 1999 average daily food supplies per capita in Sub-Saharan Africa increased a paltry 6 percent from 2,059 to 2,195 calories. The decline in food supplies in Eastern Europe and the former Soviet Union (EEFSU) after the collapse of communist regimes there only underscores the importance of economic development.

To put the improvements in per capita food supplies into context, the United Nations' Food and Agricultural Organization estimates that an adult in developing countries needs a minimum of 1,300 to 1,700 calories per day merely to keep basic metabolic activities functioning when at rest in a supine position. Food intake below those levels results in poor health, declining body weight, and physical and mental impairment. If one allows for moderate activity, then the national daily average requirement increases to between 2,000 and 2,310 calories per person.

Therefore, since 1961, developing countries' available food supply has, on average, gone from inadequate to above adequate. But these averages mask the fact that hunger still persists today since many people unfortunately have below-average food intake. Nevertheless, between 1969–71 and 1997–99 the number of people suffering from chronic undernourishment in developing countries declined from 920 million to 790 million, or from 35 percent to 17 percent of their population, despite a 76 percent growth in their population. Thus gaps between developing and developed countries in hunger and malnourishment have, in the aggregate, declined in absolute and relative terms. But the trends for Sub-Saharan Africa tell a somewhat more nuanced tale. Between 1979–81 and 1997–99, the share of population that was undernourished declined from 38 to 34 percent, but the absolute numbers increased from 168 million to 194 million.

Why does economic development reduce the level of undernourishment? Cross-country data show that both crop yield and per capita food supply . . . increase with income. Crop yields increase because richer countries (or farmers) are better able to afford yield- and productivity-enhancing technologies, such as fertilizers, pesticides, better seeds, and tractors. But even if a country has poor yields or insufficient production, if it is rich it can import its food needs. Hence, . . . the richer the country, the greater its available food supplies.

Because it is always possible to have local food shortages in the midst of a worldwide glut, the importance of trade should not be underestimated. Currently, grain imports amount to 10 percent of production in developing countries and 20 percent in Sub-Saharan Africa. Without such imports, food prices in those countries would no doubt be higher and more people would be priced out of the market. In essence, globalization, through trade, has enhanced food security. And in doing so it has reduced the severe health burdens that accompany hunger and undernourishment.

To summarize, the developing countries where hunger and undernourishment were reduced the most are those that also experienced the most economic development. Certainly, for this indicator, globalization leading to faster economic development and greater trade would seem to be the solution rather than the problem.

Infant Mortality

Before industrialization, infant mortality, measured as the number of children dying before reaching their first birthday, typically exceeded 200 per 1,000 live births. Starting in the 19th century, infant mortality began to drop in several of the currently developed countries because of advances in agriculture, nutrition, medicine, and public health. By the early 1950s, a gap had opened up between developed and developing countries as infant mortality dropped to 59 in the former and 178 in the latter. By 1998 further medical advances reduced infant mortality in developed countries to 9, but because existing health care technology (including knowledge) diffused even faster from developed to developing countries, it had declined to 64 in the latter. Thus, during the past half century the gap between developed and developing countries has been halved.

The drop in infant mortality has been broad and deep. Since at least 1960 infant mortality has dropped more or less continuously. It also illustrates that in any given year, . . . higher per capita income is generally associated with lower infant mortality. Between 1960 and 1999, the gaps in this indicator between high-income members of the Organization for Economic Cooperation and Development [OECD] and the other income groups shrank rather than increased. These gaps closed the fastest for medium-income countries and the slowest for Sub-Saharan Africa. This is counterintuitive since the larger the initial gap, the faster it ought to shrink, because the closer infant mortality is to zero, the harder it should be to reduce it further. . . .

Infant Mortality, 1960–1999

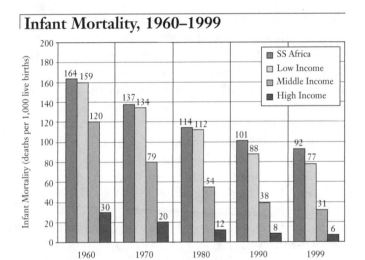

World Bank, *World Development Indicators 2001.*

Many developing countries are far better off today than the currently developed countries were at equivalent levels of economic development. In 1913 when the United States had a per capita income of $5,301 (in 1990 international dollars), its infant mortality was about 100. By contrast, in 1998 China's and India's, for example, were 31 and 71, respectively, despite per capita incomes that were 41 to 67 percent lower.

Thus, as is the case for hunger and undernourishment, the areas where infant mortality has improved the least are those with insufficient economic development or that, for whatever reason, have been unable to fully capitalize on existing knowledge and technology. Once again, globalization seems to be part of the solution rather than the problem.

Life Expectancy

Because historically the decline in infant mortality was a major factor in the improvement in life expectancy, there are certain parallels between the progress in these two indicators, especially in the earlier years.

For much of human history average life expectancy was between 20 and 30 years. Life expectancies in the currently developed countries increased slightly in the early part of the 19th century, followed by (small) declines in the middle half of the 1800s (probably because of urbanization) before commencing, with a few notable exceptions and some minor fluctuations, a sustained improvement that continues to this day.

Contributing to these improvements were increases in food supplies per capita; the ascendancy of the germ theory; and the adoption of such basic public health measures as access to clean water, sanitation, pasteurization, vaccination, antibiotics, and the use of pesticides such as DDT to control malaria and other vector-borne diseases.

Because these public health and medical advances were discovered, developed, and adopted first by the developed countries, a substantial gap opened up in average life expectancy between them and developing countries. By the early 1950s the gap stood at 25.7 years in favor of the former. But by the late 1990s, with the diffusion and transfer of technology (including knowledge) to developing countries, this gap had closed to 11.6 years. . . .

In any given year, life expectancy increases with per capita income. Between 1960 and 1999, life expectancy improved for high-income OECD and middle-income countries. However, the gap between these two sets of countries, which had shrunk from 24.5 in 1960 to 7.9 by the late 1980s, increased slightly to 8.6 by 1999, mainly because the middle-income countries include many EEFSU nations in which life expectancies declined as their economies contracted during that period.

The AIDS Epidemic

The gap between high-income OECD and low-income countries also declined for most of the post–World War II period. But it expanded slightly from 1997 to 1999 because, while life expectancy in the former continued to increase because of medical advances, it dropped slightly in the latter. This drop was particularly severe in Sub-Saharan Africa where . . . life expectancy declined by three years in the 1990s, as a result of the HIV/AIDS epidemic and—in some cases, even more important—the resurgence of malaria aggravated by civil unrest and cross-border conflicts in several areas. Consequently, the gap between rich and poor countries expanded in the 1990s, reversing the direction of the trend of previous decades. But it didn't expand because the rich increased their life expectancy at the expense of the poor; rather it was because, when faced with new diseases (such as AIDS) or new forms of ancient ones (for example, drug-resistant tuberculosis), the poor countries lacked the economic and human resources not only to develop effective treatments but also to import and adapt treatments invented and developed in the rich countries. Notably, both economic and human resources are more likely to be augmented with globalization than without it.

Sub-Saharan Africa's experience with AIDS is in stark contrast to that of the richer nations. When the disease first appeared, it resulted in almost certain death everywhere—in developed as well as developing countries. The former, particularly the United States, launched a massive assault on the disease, which led to the development of several technologies to reduce its toll. As a consequence, between 1995 and 1999 estimated U.S. deaths due to AIDS dropped by more than two-thirds (from 50,610 to 16,273) although the number of cases increased by almost half (from 216,796 to 320,282). In 1996 it was the eighth leading cause of death in the United States. By 1998 it had dropped out of the worst 15 list.

The United States was able to reduce deaths from AIDS because it both was wealthy and had the human capital to address this disease. But despite the fact that the necessary technology now exists and, in theory, is available worldwide, similar improvements have yet to occur in Sub-Saharan countries because they cannot afford the cost of treatment, unless it is subsidized by the governments, charities, or even industries of the *richer* nations. And indeed such subsidies are exactly what the worldwide effort to contain HIV/AIDS hopes to mobilize. This is as clear an illustration as any that the greater the economic resources, the greater the likelihood not only of creating new technologies but, equally important, of actually putting those technologies to use. And unless technologies are used, they will sit as curios on a shelf, providing no benefit to humanity. . . .

Child Labor

The proportion of children in the workforce has also been declining steadily for each of the income groups, and the richer the group, the lower that percentage. Gaps in child labor between Sub-Saharan Africa, the low- and middle-income countries, and the high-income OECD countries have been shrinking at least since 1960. For this indicator also, the gap between high-income OECD and middle-income countries has diminished the most; the gap between the former and Sub-Saharan Africa has diminished the least. . . .

Summarizing the Trends

The well-being of the vast majority of the world's population has improved and continues to improve. Because of a combination of economic growth and technological change, compared to a half century ago the average person today lives longer and is less hungry, healthier, more educated, and more likely to have children in a schoolroom than in the workplace. During that period, indicators of well-being have improved for every country group, although life expectancies have declined in many Sub-Saharan and EEFSU countries since the late 1980s because of HIV/AIDS, malaria, or problems related to economic deterioration.

For every indicator examined, regardless of whether the rich are richer and the poor poorer, gaps in human well-being between the rich countries and other income groups have for the most part shrunk over the past four decades. However, comparing rich countries and Sub-Saharan Africa, although the gap in infant mortality between the two has continued to close, the gap in life expectancy has expanded in the past decade or so (but not enough to erase the large improvement made previously). Despite this, in aggregate, the corresponding gap in HDI [Human Development Index] has decreased.

> *"The greatest threat before humanity today is the possibility of secret and sudden attack with chemical or biological or radiological or nuclear weapons."*

Weapons of Mass Destruction Threaten Humanity's Future

George W. Bush

In the hands of terrorists and outlaw regimes, weapons of mass destruction (WMDs) are a serious threat to the future of humanity, claims U.S. president George W. Bush in the following viewpoint. During the Cold War, Bush asserts, only the world's most powerful nations had WMDs, and deterrence was sufficient to prevent their use. Today, however, black-market dealers make it easy for terrorists and failing states to acquire, build, and transport WMDs, he maintains.

As you read, consider the following questions:

1. How does Bush plan to confront the threat of WMDs at their source?
2. What strategies does the author propose to deal with dangerous regimes that build WMDs?
3. What commitments in the war on terror does the author claim are inseparable?

George W. Bush, address at National Defense University, Washington, DC, February 11, 2004.

On September the 11th, 2001, America and the world witnessed a new kind of war. We saw the great harm that a stateless network could inflict upon our country, killers armed with box cutters, mace, and 19 airline tickets. Those attacks also raised the prospect of even worse dangers—of other weapons in the hands of other men. The greatest threat before humanity today is the possibility of secret and sudden attack with chemical or biological or radiological or nuclear weapons.

In the past, enemies of America required massed armies, and great navies, powerful air forces to put our nation, our people, our friends and allies at risk. In the Cold War, Americans lived under the threat of weapons of mass destruction, but believed that deterrents made those weapons a last resort. What has changed in the 21st century is that, in the hands of terrorists, weapons of mass destruction would be a first resort—the preferred means to further their ideology of suicide and random murder. These terrible weapons are becoming easier to acquire, build, hide, and transport. Armed with a single vial of a biological agent or a single nuclear weapon, small groups of fanatics, or failing states, could gain the power to threaten great nations, threaten the world peace.

America, and the entire civilized world, will face this threat for decades to come. We must confront the danger with open eyes, and unbending purpose. I have made clear to all the policy of this nation: America will not permit terrorists and dangerous regimes to threaten us with the world's most deadly weapons.

Changing Strategies

Meeting this duty has required changes in thinking and strategy. Doctrines designed to contain empires, deter aggressive states, and defeat massed armies cannot fully protect us from this new threat. America faces the possibility of catastrophic attack from ballistic missiles armed with weapons of mass destruction. So that is why we are developing and deploying missile defenses to guard our people. The best intelligence is necessary to win the war on terror and to stop proliferation. So that is why I have established a commission that will examine our intelligence capabilities and recommend ways to improve and adapt them to detect new and emerging threats.

"Dirty pictures?... dirty plutonium 239?..."

We're determined to confront those threats at the source. We will stop these weapons from being acquired or built. We'll block them from being transferred. We'll prevent them from ever being used. One source of these weapons is dangerous and secretive regimes that build weapons of mass destruction to intimidate their neighbors and force their influence upon the world. These nations pose different challenges; they require different strategies.

Paths of Proliferation

The former dictator of Iraq possessed and used weapons of mass destruction against his own people. For 12 years, he defied the will of the international community. He refused to disarm or account for his illegal weapons and programs. He doubted our resolve to enforce our word—and now he sits in a prison cell, while his country moves toward a democratic future.

To Iraq's east, the government of Iran is unwilling to abandon a uranium enrichment program capable of producing material for nuclear weapons. The United States is working with our allies and the International Atomic Energy Agency to ensure that Iran meets its commitments and does not develop nuclear weapons.

In the Pacific, North Korea has defied the world, has tested long-range ballistic missiles, admitted its possession of nuclear weapons, and now threatens to build more. Together with our partners in Asia, America is insisting that North Korea completely, verifiably, and irreversibly dismantle its nuclear programs.

America has consistently brought these threats to the attention of international organizations. We're using every means of diplomacy to answer them. As for my part, I will continue to speak clearly on these threats. I will continue to call upon the world to confront these dangers, and to end them.

In recent years, another path of proliferation has become clear, as well. America and other nations are learning more about black-market operatives who deal in equipment and expertise related to weapons of mass destruction. These dealers are motivated by greed, or fanaticism, or both. They find eager customers in outlaw regimes, which pay millions for the parts and plans they need to speed up their weapons programs. And with deadly technology and expertise going on the market, there's the terrible possibility that terrorists groups could obtain the ultimate weapons they desire most. . . .

A Coalition to Oppose Weapons of Mass Destruction

We're adjusting our strategies to the threats of a new era. America and the nations of Australia, France and Germany, Italy and Japan, the Netherlands, Poland, Portugal, Spain and the United Kingdom have launched the Proliferation Security Initiative [PSI] to interdict lethal materials in transit. Our nations are sharing intelligence information, tracking suspect international cargo, conducting joint military exercises. We're prepared to search planes and ships, to seize weapons and missiles and equipment that raise proliferation concerns, just as we did in stopping the dangerous cargo on the *BBC China* before it reached Libya. Three more governments—Canada and Singapore and Norway—will be participating in this initiative. We'll continue to expand the core group of PSI countries. And as PSI grows, proliferators will find it harder than ever to trade in illicit weapons.

There is a consensus among nations that proliferation cannot be tolerated. Yet this consensus means little unless it is translated into action. Every civilized nation has a stake in preventing the spread of weapons of mass destruction. These materials and technologies, and the people who traffic in them, cross many borders. To stop this trade, the nations of the world must be strong and determined. We must work together, we must act effectively. . . .

As we move forward to address these challenges we will consult with our friends and allies on all these new measures. We will listen to their ideas. Together we will defend the safety of all nations and preserve the peace of the world.

[Since 2001] a great coalition has come together to defeat terrorism and to oppose the spread of weapons of mass destruction—the inseparable commitments of the war on terror. We've shown that proliferators can be discovered and can be stopped. We've shown that for regimes that choose defiance, there are serious consequences. The way ahead is not easy, but it is clear. We will proceed as if the lives of our citizens depend on our vigilance, because they do. Terrorists and terror states are in a race for weapons of mass murder, a race they must lose. Terrorists are resourceful; we're more resourceful. They're determined; we must be more determined. We will never lose focus or resolve. We'll be unrelenting in the defense of free nations, and rise to the hard demands of dangerous times.

"Despite all of the government hoopla surrounding weapons of mass destruction prior to and subsequent to September 11, the threat has been hyped."

The Threat from Weapons of Mass Destruction Is Exaggerated

Ivan Eland

The threat posed by weapons of mass destruction (WMDs) has been overstated, argues Ivan Eland in the following viewpoint. Chemical and biological weapons, he claims, have rarely been effective since they depend on favorable weather conditions to work. Nuclear weapons, he asserts, are difficult to build, requiring scientific experts and expensive infrastructure, so terrorists are unlikely to have them. Moreover, deterrence will continue to be effective in preventing the use of nuclear weapons; the United States, which still has the largest nuclear arsenal, could easily destroy rogue states that may use them, he maintains. Eland is a fellow at the Independent Institute, a nonpartisan think tank.

As you read, consider the following questions:

1. In Eland's opinion, what is important to remember during propaganda campaigns preceding future U.S. invasions?
2. According to the author, why do rogue states have no incentive to give costly nuclear weapons to terrorists?

Ivan Eland, "Weapons of Mass Destruction Are Overrated as a Threat to America," www.independentinstitute.com, January 2004. Copyright © 2004 by The Independent Institute, 100 Swan Way, Oakland, CA 94621-1428 USA. info@independent.org; www.independent.org; www.independent.org/newsroom/article.asp?id=1256.

David Kay, [George Bush's] handpicked weapons of mass destruction snoop in Iraq, has resigned and criticized U.S. intelligence for not realizing that Iraqi weapons programs were in disarray. He now thinks that the stocks of chemical and biological weapons were destroyed in the 1990s—out of fear that U.N. [United Nations] weapons inspectors would discover them—and that new production was not initiated. He also believes that Iraq's nuclear program had been restarted but was only at a very primitive stage—hardly the imminent threat alleged by the Bush administration as a justification for immediate war. So with the final nail being driven into the coffin of the administration's main rationale for war against Iraq, Iraqi weapons programs are not the only things in disarray. After Kay's initial comments, Secretary of State Colin Powell had to admit that the Iraqi government may no longer have had such arms.

Unraveling Propaganda Campaigns

Perhaps Kay's findings will finally cause the American public to heed the Iraq war critics' call to hold the administration accountable for the deaths of more than 500 American service personnel and countless innocent Iraqis (which, strangely, the American government cannot seem to estimate). But let's not hold our breath. The September 11 [2001, terrorist attacks] gave the Bush administration body armor that is only now developing chinks. And Kay's findings help debunk the Iraqi threat but may actually cloud other issues. First, Kay blames U.S. intelligence for not realizing that Iraq's weapons programs were in shambles. This conclusion is valid, but fits into the administration's desire to scapegoat U.S. spy agencies to hide its own twisting and embellishing of the already faulty intelligence information.

Second and important to remember during propaganda campaigns preceding any future invasions of "axis of evil"[1] nations: despite all of the government hoopla surrounding weapons of mass destruction [WMDs] prior to and subsequent to September 11, the threat has been hyped. Prior to

1. President George W. Bush has called Iran, Iraq, and North Korea the "Axis of Evil."

the invasion of Iraq, the Department of Defense noted "extant and emerging threats" from 12 nations with nuclear programs, 13 countries with biological weapons, and 16 nations with chemical weapons.

Understanding Weapons of Mass Destruction

Although nuclear, chemical and biological weapons usually fall under the scary (it's done on purpose) WMD label, only nuclear weapons should be in that category. (As the September 11 attacks showed, high casualties could be inflicted without using WMD.) Chemical weapons have a much smaller area of contamination than do biological and nuclear arms and historically have been less deadly than even conventional bombs. Chemical weapons are best employed by the defending side—if the attacking side uses them, friendly troops would likely have to advance through the gas. Although chemical weapons are probably the easiest of the three to produce, [terrorist group] al Qaeda's efforts to date have been very crude. Some infrastructure is needed to produce chemical weapons so detection of production may be possible.

Terrorists Are Unlikely to Use Nuclear Weapons

The materials needed to make a nuclear bomb do not occur in significant quantities in nature, and making them is so difficult as to be well beyond the plausible capabilities of terrorist groups. Hence, if the world community can effectively guard all of the existing stockpiles, it can prevent nuclear weapons terrorism from ever occurring: no material, no bomb.

Nuclear Threat Initiative, 2002.

Although biological weapons are better for terrorizing civilian populations than for battlefield use (they take effect slowly and the battle probably will be over by then), weaponizing biological agents takes a great deal of scientific expertise. Aum Shinrikyo, a well-funded Japanese terror group, hired scientists to do so but was unsuccessful. Although small pox could cause casualties on the scale of a nuclear detonation, only a few countries have the virus. A successful attack with either chemical or biological weapons is heavily dependent on favorable weather conditions. Missiles are not the ideal delivery systems for either type of weapon because the agent can be incinerated by heat from the explosive impact.

No one would argue that nuclear weapons are incapable of causing mass destruction. But building nuclear weapons requires a large infrastructure, scientists, engineers and strictly controlled fissile material (plutonium or enriched uranium). Terrorists are probably not capable of building even a crude nuclear weapon. Many countries aren't either. Iraq and Libya both failed to get such weapons.

But some clearly undesirable governments—for example, North Korea—eventually may get nuclear weapons and the long-range missiles to deliver them to the United States. North Korea always has been a bigger WMD threat than Iraq. But the United States could rely on its world dominant nuclear arsenal to deter attacks from the small arsenals of nascent nuclear powers, rather than conducting unnecessary preventative invasions. The United States took this route when the totalitarian Soviet Union and the even more radical Maoist China were developing nuclear weapons. Deterrence has worked in the past and will most likely work in the future because the remaining destitute "rogue", states have home addresses that could be wiped off the map—albeit with massive casualties—with thousands of U.S. nuclear warheads. Moreover, even though those nations disagree with intrusive U.S. foreign policy in their regions, they have no incentive to give such costly weapons to unpredictable terrorist groups. If such assistance were discovered, the superpower might be motivated to incinerate their countries. Before the war, the president's own CIA [Central Intelligence Agency] reported that Iraq would be unlikely to use WMD or give them to terrorists unless the United States invaded.

Although the unnecessary and continuing deaths of Americans and Iraqis are tragic, most alarming for the republic may have been the absence of public outcry to halt the administration's rush into a war that its own intelligence agency predicted would be counterproductive.

> *"The threat posed by growing food insecurity may dwarf [terrorism] in terms of the number of lives lost and the extent of economic disruption."*

Food Scarcity Is a Serious Threat to Global Security

Lester Brown

Food scarcity threatens global political stability and economic security, asserts Lester Brown in the following excerpt from his book *Outgrowing the Earth: The Food Security Challenge in an Age of Falling Water Tables and Rising Temperatures*. While the world's population grows, food production has slowed due to rising temperatures, a depleted water supply, and out-of-date agricultural techniques, he maintains. When food production slows, Brown argues, prices rise, making food scarce in poor countries. Food scarcity leads to political instability, which in turn threatens global economic progress, he claims. Brown is founder and president of the Earth Policy Institute, an environmental advocacy organization.

As you read, consider the following questions:

1. In what parts of the world is most of the population growth expected to occur, in Brown's view?
2. In the author's opinion, what issues become important when the world moves into a period dominated by grain shortages, not surpluses?
3. According to the author, future food security depends on stabilizing what four key agricultural resources?

Lester Brown, *Outgrowing the Earth: The Food Security Challenge in an Age of Falling Water Tables and Rising Temperatures*. Washington, DC: Earth Policy Institute, 2004. Copyright © 2004 by the Earth Policy Institute. Reproduced by permission.

In each of the first four years of this new century, world grain production has fallen short of consumption. The shortfalls in 2002 and 2003, the largest on record, and the smaller ones in 2000 and 2001 were covered by drawing down stocks. These four consecutive shortfalls in the world grain harvest have dropped stocks to their lowest level in 30 years.

When there are no longer any stocks to draw down, the only option will be to reduce consumption.

In early 2004, world grain prices were up some 20 percent over previous years. Soybean prices were double the levels of a year earlier. The combination of stronger prices at planting time and the best weather in a decade raised the 2004 grain harvest by 124 million tons to 1,965 million tons, up 7 percent. For the first time in five years, production matched consumption, but only barely. Even with this exceptional harvest, the world was still unable to rebuild depleted grain stocks.

The immediate question is, Will the 2005 harvest be sufficient to meet growing world demand, or will it again fall short? If the latter, then world grain stocks will drop to their lowest level ever—and the world will be in uncharted territory on the food front.

The risk is that another large shortfall could drive prices off the top of the chart, leading to widespread political instability in low-income countries that import part of their grain. Such political instability could disrupt global economic progress, forcing world leaders to recognize that they can no longer neglect the population and environmental trends that have created harvest shortfalls in four out of the last five years.

While terrorism will no doubt remain an important policy issue, the threat posed by growing food insecurity may dwarf it in terms of the number of lives lost and the extent of economic disruption.

A Tighter Supply

The world food supply is tightening because world grain demand is continuing to expand at a robust pace while production growth is slowing as the backlog of unused agricultural technology shrinks, cropland is converted to non-farm uses, rising temperatures shrink harvests, aquifers are depleted, and irrigation water is diverted to cities.

The world's population is projected to increase by nearly three billion by 2050. Two-thirds of this growth will occur in the Indian subcontinent and in Africa, the world's hungriest regions. Most of the other one billion people will be born in the Middle East, which faces a doubling of its population, and in Latin America, Southeast Asia, and the United States. This projected population increase requires more land not only to produce food but also for living space—homes, factories, offices, schools, and roads. . . .

In many countries, the irrigation water supply is shrinking as aquifers are depleted. But even as wells are going dry, irrigation water is being diverted to fast-growing cities. Farmers are getting a smaller share of a diminishing supply. Perhaps even more importantly, . . . research indicates that higher temperatures reduce grain harvests; this at a time when we face the prospect of continually rising temperatures.

In contrast to the last half-century, when the world fish catch quintupled to reach 93 million tons, we cannot expect any growth in the fish catch at all during the next half-century. The growing world demand for seafood must now be satisfied entirely from aquaculture, where fish are fed mostly grain and soymeal. This puts additional pressure on the earth's land and water resources.

Beyond the various environmental and resource trends that are affecting the food prospect, the world's farmers are now also wrestling with a shrinking backlog of agricultural technology. For the world's more progressive farmers, there are few, if any, unused technologies that will substantially raise land productivity. Even more serious, dramatic new yield-raising technologies are likely to be few and far between.

The Politics of Food Scarcity

For more than 40 years, international trade negotiations have been dominated by grain-exporting countries—principally the United States, Canada, Argentina, and Australia—pressing for greater access to markets in importing countries. Now the world may be moving into a period dominated not by surpluses but by shortages. In this case, the issue becomes not exporters' access to markets but importers' access to supplies. . . .

China's rice crop shortfall in 2004 of 10 million tons hung over the world market like a sword of Damocles. Where the rice would come from was not clear. The big test of the international community's capacity to manage scarcity may come when China turns to the world market for massive imports of 30, 40, or 50 million tons of grain per year—demand on a scale that could quickly overwhelm world grain markets. When this happens, China will have to look to the United States, which controls nearly half the world's grain exports.

This will pose a fascinating geopolitical situation: 1.3 billion Chinese consumers, who have a $120 billion trade surplus with the United States—enough to buy the entire U.S. grain harvest twice—will be competing with us for our grain, driving up food prices. In such a situation 30 years ago, the United States would simply have restricted exports, but today it has a stake in a politically stable China. The Chinese economy is not only the engine powering the Asian economy, it is also the only large economy worldwide that has maintained a full head of steam in recent years. Managing this flow of grain so as to satisfy the needs of consumers in both countries may become one of the leading foreign policy challenges of this new century.

How exporting countries make room for China's vast needs in their export allocations will help determine how the world addresses the stresses associated with outgrowing the Earth. How low-income, importing countries fare in this competition for grain will also tell us something about future political stability. And, finally, how the United States responds to China's growing demands for grain even as it drives up grain and food prices for U.S. consumers will tell us much about the shape of the new world order.

A New Definition of Famine

One reason food shortages do not get the attention they once did is because famine, in effect, has been redefined. At one time, famine was a geographic phenomenon. When a country or region had a poor harvest, its people often faced famine. Given the growing integration of the world grain economy and today's capacity to move grain around the world, famine is concentrated much less in specific geographic regions and much more among income groups. Food shortages now translate into higher worldwide prices that affect low-income people throughout the world, forcing many to try to tighten their belts when there are no more notches left.

In the event of life-threatening grain price rises, a tax on livestock products could help alleviate temporary shortages. This would reduce consumption of grain-fed livestock products—meat, milk, and eggs—and thus free up for human consumption a small share of the grain normally fed to livestock and poultry. In the United States, a reduction in grain consumption per person from 800 to 700 kilograms by moving down the food chain somewhat would not only leave most U.S. citizens healthier, it would also reduce grain consumption by some 30 million tons. That would be enough to feed 150 million people in low-income countries. At a time when grain stocks are at an all-time low and the risk of dramatic price jumps is higher than at any time in a generation, a tax on livestock products is the one safety cushion that could be used to buy time to stabilize population and restore economic stability in the world food economy.

Stabilizing the Resource Base

Future food security depends on stabilizing four key agricultural resources: cropland, water, rangeland, and the Earth's climate system. Stabilizing the farmland base means protecting it from both soil erosion and the conversion to non-farm uses. Protecting water resources means stabilizing water tables. The overdrafting that lowers water tables also raises the energy used for pumping. For example, in some states in India half of all electricity is used for water pumping. Higher pumping costs ultimately mean higher food production costs.

Protecting rangeland is an integral part of the food security formula not only because damage to rangeland from overgrazing reduces the livestock carrying capacity, but also because the dust storms that follow de-vegetation of the land can disrupt economic activity hundreds of miles away. The drifting sand that follows the conversion of rangeland to desert can also invade farming areas, rendering cultivation impossible.

Most importantly, we need to stabilize the climate system.

Agriculture as we know it has evolved over 11,000 years of rather remarkable climate stability. The negative effect of higher temperatures on grain yields underlines the importance of stabilizing the climate as quickly as possible.

Stabilizing any one of these resources is demanding, but our generation faces the need to do all four at the same time. This is a demanding undertaking in terms of leadership time and energy and also in financial terms. Desert remediation in China alone will require estimated expenditures of some $28 billion.

The Relationship Between Land and Food Scarcity

In the early 1960s, only four countries—Kuwait, Singapore, Oman and Japan—had insufficient arable land to feed their populations without highly intensive agriculture, but they were wealthy enough to either import food or increase agricultural productivity with modern farming methods. By 1990, the number of countries with scarcity of arable land had risen to nine, and included the Netherlands, South Korea and Egypt. By 2025, however, at least 17 additional countries are projected to join the ranks of countries suffering from a scarcity of arable land, among them some of the world's poorest nations: Somalia, Bangladesh, Kenya, Mauritania, and Yemen.

Population Action International, www.populationaction.org, April 15, 1995.

It may seem obvious that if water tables start to fall and wells begin to go dry, alarm bells would ring and governments would launch an immediate effort to reduce pumping and bring demand into balance with supply by adopting water conservation measures. But not one of the scores of countries where water levels are falling has succeeded in stabilizing its water tables.

Protecting the world's grainland is equally difficult. Advancing deserts are a formidable threat in countries such as Mexico, Nigeria, Algeria, Iran, Kazakhstan, India, and China. If governments continue to treat the symptoms of desertification and fail to address the root causes, such as continuing population growth and excessive livestock numbers, the deserts will continue to advance.

Shielding cropland from non-farm demands can also be politically complex. The cropland-consuming trends that are an integral part of the modernization process, such as building roads, housing, and factories, are difficult to arrest, much less reverse. And yet the world as a whole cannot continue indefinitely to lose cropland without eventually facing serious trouble on the food front.

A Complex Challenge

Diminishing returns are setting in on several fronts, including the quality of new land that can be brought under the plow, the production response to additional fertilizer applications, the opportunity for drilling new irrigation wells, and the potential of research investments to produce technologies that will boost production dramatically.

In 1950, opportunities for expanding the cultivated area were already limited, but there were still some to be found here and there. Together, they helped expand the world grainland area by roughly one-fifth. Today, in contrast, the only country that has the potential to increase the world grainland area measurably is Brazil. And doing this would raise numerous environmental questions, ranging from soil erosion to decreased carbon sequestration in the plowed areas.

A half-century ago, every country in the world could anticipate using much more fertilizer. Today, using more fertilizer has little effect on production in many countries. And a half-century ago, the use of underground water for irrigation was almost nonexistent. Vast aquifers were waiting to be tapped, yielding a sustainable supply of irrigation water. Today, drilling more irrigation wells is likely only to hasten the depletion of aquifers and a resulting drop in food production.

Diminishing returns also affect agricultural research. Fifty years ago, agricultural scientists were just beginning to adapt the high-yielding dwarf wheats and rices and the hybrid corn to widely varying growing conditions around the world. Today, the plant breeding focus has shifted from raising yields to using biotechnology to develop varieties that are insect-resistant or herbicide-tolerant. Plant breeding advances may still raise yields five percent here or perhaps 15 percent there, but the potential for dramatic gains appears limited.

The world has changed in other ways. As world population and the global economy expanded dramatically over the last half-century, the world quietly moved into a new era, one in which the economy began pressing against the earth's natural limits. In this new situation, activities in one economic sector can affect another. Historically, for example, what happened in the transport sector had little effect on agriculture. But in a world with 6.3 billion people, most of whom would like to own a car, auto-centered transport systems will consume a vast area of cropland.

If densely populated countries like China and India turn to cars as the primary means of transportation, they will pit affluent automobile owners against low-income food consumers in the competition for land. These nations simply do not have enough land to support hundreds of millions of cars and to feed their people.

We can no longer take population projections as a given. The world cannot afford for any woman to be without family planning advice and contraceptives. Today, however, an estimated 137 million women want to limit the size of their families but lack access to the family planning services needed to do so. Eradicating hunger depends on filling the family planning gap and creating the social conditions that will accelerate the shift to smaller families.

Food Security and Water

Food security is affected not only by the food:population equation, but also by the water:population equation and the efforts of water resource ministries to raise water productivity. Indeed, since 70 percent of world water use is for irrigation, eradicating hunger may now depend on a global full-court press to raise water productivity. Everyone knows it takes water to produce food, but we often do not realize how water intensive food production is and how quickly water shortages can translate into food shortages. The ministry of health and family planning needs to cooperate not only with the ministry of agriculture but also with the ministry of water resources. Those living in land hungry, water-short countries need to know how their childbearing decisions will affect the next generation's access to water and to food.

One of the essentials for success in this new situation is strong political leaders. In the absence of competent leaders who understand the complex interaction of these issues, the cooperation needed to ensure a country's future food security may simply not be forthcoming. In the absence of such leadership, a deterioration in the food situation may be unavoidable.

A Global Issue

In a world that is increasingly integrated economically, food security is now a global issue. In an integrated world grain market, everyone is affected by the same price shifts. A doubling of grain prices, which is a distinct possibility if we cannot accelerate the growth in grain production, could impoverish more people and destabilize more governments than any event in history. Our future depends on working together to avoid a destabilizing jump in world food prices. Everyone has a stake in stabilizing the agricultural resource base. Everyone has a stake in securing future food supplies. We all have a responsibility to work for the policies—whether in agriculture, energy, population, water use, cropland protection, or soil conservation—that will help ensure future world food security.

The complexity of the challenges the world is facing is matched by the enormity of the effort required to reverse the trends that are undermining future food security. Halting the advancing deserts in China, arresting the fall in water tables in India, and reversing the rise in carbon emissions in the United States are essential. Each will require a strong, new initiative—one that demands a wartime sense of urgency and leadership.

We have inherited the mindset, policies, and fiscal priorities from an era of food security that no longer exists. The policies that once provided food security will no longer suffice in a world where we are pressing against the sustainable yields of oceanic fisheries and underground aquifers and the limits of nature to fix carbon dioxide. Unless we recognize the nature of the era we are entering and adopt new policies and priorities that recognize the Earth's natural limits, world food security could begin to deteriorate. If it does, food security could quickly eclipse terrorism as the overriding concern of governments.

"Cultural globalization . . . destroys diversity and displaces the opportunity to sustain decent human life through an assortment of many different cultures."

The Spread of Western Culture Threatens Local Cultures

Wole Akande

According to Wole Akande in the following viewpoint, the spread of Western culture is undermining the well-being of non-Western nations. Countries that have already seen their cultures change as a result of centuries of Western colonization are particularly vulnerable, Akande asserts. People who lose their cultures also lose their sense of who they are and what values they respect, leading to cultural and political instability, he asserts. Akande, a freelance journalist, maintains a Nigerian community Web site.

As you read, consider the following questions:
1. According to Akande, what Western values are people of the non-Western world absorbing?
2. In the author's opinion, what is the driving force of today's economic globalization?
3. What has happened to the role of local culture, in the author's view?

Wole Akande, "The Drawbacks of Cultural Globalization," *Yellow Times,* November 10, 2002. Copyright © 2002 by Wole Akande. Reproduced by permission.

The aggressive spread of market economics and communication technologies—often under the control of Western multinationals—brings new challenges to local cultures and values in Africa and other non-Western societies. Sometimes it seems as if a tidal wave of the worst Western culture is creeping across the globe like a giant strawberry milkshake oozing over the planet, with a flavor that is distinctly sweet, sickly and manifestly homogenous.

Suddenly, people all over Africa and the rest of the non-Westernized regions of the world, appear to be imbibing materialistic and individualistic values previously associated with Western culture. What explains this apparently abrupt Westernization? One major reason is the structural change in the world economy: globalization and the flood of goods dumped in poor countries that are marketed by mass seductive advertising which is blatantly superficial but nonetheless successful in creating fresh desires in peoples of traditional societies.

Undermining Non-Western Cultures

For some, especially the young, these new products and content with new ideas can be exhilarating. Change may mean escape from oppressive traditions. It may also bring new opportunities for cultures to mingle in creative ways. Obviously, it would be an excessive form of cultural fundamentalism to suggest that Africans should try to keep everything exactly as it is, rather than allowing culture to develop. However, there is genuine cause for concern about the rate at which cultures (African and non-African) are being undermined in a world that is bound together by ever-stronger economic ties.

Starting in the sixteenth century, Western adventurers made a conscious effort to undermine the cultural heritage of various peoples around the world; this has been accomplished by imposing Western religion and cultural practices on those with a different way of life.

Justified initially as a civilizing mission and subsequently dubbed modernization, in practice it was wholesale Westernization with very little room for any viable middle ground. For instance, in the 19th century, Abeokuta (a town in West Africa), inspired by its Western educated former slaves, responded to the challenges of these pervasive foreign influences with a unique form of defensive modernization and reform which eventually crumbled under the weight of the overwhelming imperial British power. Accordingly, until the late twentieth century, it was assumed that development for the colonized peoples must involve a denial of their history, a rejection of their cultural heritage and the adoption of Western cultural practices.

The effect of this policy in the case of Africa, as Professor [B.W.] Andah once noted, was untold damage to the African psyche, "so much so that most Africans have come to believe as truth, the myths and lies about them as being primitive, history-less, mindless, cursed, lazy, inherently evil and corrupt, third world, underdeveloped."

Cultural Disorientation

In short, today, African culture has been decimated. More importantly, colonialism paved the way for today's cultural globalization by leaving the colonized in a state of cultural disorientation and consequently vulnerable to continuing cultural invasion. This disorientation manifests itself in one or two extreme forms:

1. exaggerated attachment to an often reinvented past in the name of tradition and culture; or
2. attempts at wholesale adoption of anything and everything foreign.

It may sound extreme but academic language studies have proven that particular aspects of culture can and do disappear forever; even optimistic estimates suggest that as many as 90 percent of the world's languages will disappear in the next century.

While an important feature of globalization today is its de-Westernization (with the emergence of some non-Western nations—like Japan—as key actors), the reality is that in many important respects, Western culture (some would say American culture) remains the domineering force in the world today. Western culture fuels globalization today and, as it did during the age of imperialism and colonization, helps to reinforce the hegemony of the West. Information technology, as the driving force of economic globalization, has also become a veritable instrument for propagating Western culture.

Commercialization of Culture

Perhaps by far the most important far-reaching effect of cultural globalization is the commercialization of culture. Production and consumption of cultural goods and services have become commodities, along with the essentials of social life (marriage and family life, religion, work and leisure), that are the crucibles of cultural creation. In a way very similar to economic globalization, most people (and especially the poor) do not experience cultural globalization on terms they have decided for themselves. Culture—whether it is music, food, clothes, art, sport, images of age or youth, masculinity or femininity—has become a product, sold in the market place. As the former chairman of Coca-Cola, Robert Goizueta, said: "People around the world are today connected by brand-name consumer products as much as by anything else."

A War on Culture

Globalization is a declaration of war upon all other cultures. And in cultural wars, there is no exemption for civilians; there are no innocent bystanders. Why should it be expected that ancient and rooted civilizations are going to accept this peripheralisation without a struggle? The answer to that is that globalization carries an implicit promise that it will relieve poverty and offer security—perhaps the most ancient of human dreams. Because of the power of global capitalism to create wealth, it is assumed that this priority must sweep aside all other human preoccupations, including all existing institutions, interpretations and searches for meaning in the world.

Jeremy Seabrook, *Korea Herald*, January 13, 2004.

The commercialization of culture has a disturbing impact on people. What once was an element of their way of life becomes a product, rather than something unique they had made to suit their own specific needs and circumstances. At the same time, people are increasingly bombarded with new images, new music, new clothes and new values. The familiar and old are to be discarded. While there was cultural change long before globalization, there is a danger that much will be lost simply because it is not valued by global markets. "In Ghana [West Africa]," says Siapha Kamara, formerly of the Ecumenical Training and Consultancy Centre, "traditional values have been overtaken by Coca-Cola culture. The Michael Jackson style of music and culture is taking over and we don't have the values to cope with it."

Consequently, it has been observed, globalized "cultural" industries are taking over traditional forms of creation and dissemination of culture. Local culture's role as a spontaneous and integral part of people's life is eroded and it ceases to serve as the means of constructing societal values, reproducing group identity and building social cohesion. The end result becomes global integration at the expense of local disintegration.

As with other markets, the players of the cultural market place are unevenly matched. Global media is increasingly in the hands of a few, large, powerful organizations, as is the production of music and film. For example, by 1997, the MTV television station was available to 280 million households in over 70 countries. Fearing a loss of viewers, local television stations in many African countries have filled their transmissions with cost effective Western produced shows, superficial news broadcasts, quiz shows and, of course, advertisements. Consequently, TV programs all over the world resemble each other more and more and so do the products in the field of music, film industry and publishing companies.

Undermining Existing Values

The common aspect of the globalized culture is that it pursues the same "one size fits all" ideal: the archetypical middle-class family according to the American model in which consumerism is the norm. The result of this cultural process of homogenization is that a large section of the world's population dreams of living like Cosby & Co. or like the characters in any other stereotyped American soap opera. In addition, the dream of living a better life causes thousands of people to move to already overcrowded cities like Lagos, Nigeria's sprawling commercial capital; this city has grown from a population of 18,000 in 1901 to over 12 million in 2001. The majority of these new immigrants end up in slum quarters leading to poverty, pollution and misery.

Such a radical undermining of people's existing values and

cultures has a corrosive impact on their sense of who they are, what they want and what they respect. It attacks spiritual values and faith traditions. The cumulative effect in Africa is a crisis of cultural confidence, combined with the increased economic uncertainty and crime which global integration often brings. This creates real problems for social solidarity, whether it is at the level of nation, community or family. While it offers shiny new goods as compared to old faded ones, the market offers no replacement for such community solidarity.

In conclusion, cultural globalization, or worldwide McDonaldization, destroys diversity and displaces the opportunity to sustain decent human life through an assortment of many different cultures. It is more a consequence of power concentration in the global media and manufacturing companies than the people's own wish to abandon their cultural identity and diversity.

Periodical Bibliography

The following articles have been selected to supplement the diverse views presented in this chapter.

Tamim Ansary	"A War Won't End Terrorism," *San Francisco Chronicle*, October 19, 2002.
Michelle Bata and Albert J. Bergensen	"Global Inequality: An Introduction," *Journal of World-Systems Research*, Winter 2003.
Bulletin of the Atomic Scientists	"It's Seven Minutes to Midnight," March/April 2002.
Sheldon Danziger and Deborah Reed	"Winners and Losers: The Era of Inequality Continues," *Foresight*, 2000.
Ivan Eland	"Evidence That the U.S. May Be Losing the Global War on Terror," Independent Institute, April 25, 2005.
Samuel Francis	"Spreading Democracy Is a False and Dangerous Idea," *Chronicles*, November 15, 2003.
Jonathan Granoff	"Power over the Ultimate Evil," *Tikkun*, November/December 2003.
Eric J. Hobsbawm	"Spreading Democracy," *Foreign Policy*, September/October 2004.
Jacob G. Hornberger	"The Endless War on Terrorism," Future of Freedom Foundation, September 2004.
Matt Mellen	"Who Is Getting Fed?" *Seedling*, April 2003.
Todd J. Moss	"Is Wealthier Really Healthier? *Foreign Policy*, March/April 2005.
Joseph Nye	"Globalization Is Not Americanization," *Taipei Times*, October 22, 2004.
Linda Rothstein, Catherine Auer, and Jonas Siegel	"Rethinking Doomsday: Loose Nukes, Nanobots, Smallpox, Oh My!" *Bulletin of the Atomic Scientists*, November/December 2004.
Jeremy Seabrook	"Localizing Cultures," *Korea Herald*, January 13, 2004.
Jonathan Steele	"A War That Can Never Be Won," *Guardian*, November 22, 2003.
Steven Weinberg	"Nuclear Terror: Ambling Toward Apocalypse," *Federation of American Scientists*, Summer 2003.
Western Catholic Reporter	"Democracy Takes Work, Time," April 21, 2003.

For Further Discussion

Chapter 1

1. The authors in this chapter disagree on the impact several technologies will have on humanity's future. What commonalities among the viewpoints on each side of the debate can you find in this chapter? Explain, citing from the viewpoints.

2. Michael G. Zey sees the pursuit of technology as humanity's destiny. Don Closson believes that the pursuit of some technologies usurps the power of God. How are the authors' institutional affiliations reflected in their viewpoints? Does this influence which argument you find more persuasive? Explain.

3. Ronald Bailey believes that society can prevent the abuse of genetic enhancement. Bill McKibben does not share Bailey's confidence in society, believing that genetic enhancement appeals to humanity's superficial desires. What genetic enhancements do you think would meet Bailey's reasonable-person standard and to which do you think McKibben might object?

4. Charles T. Maxwell claims that in the future oil production will no longer meet demand, resulting in an energy crisis. David Deming maintains that history is replete with such predictions and that, despite them, humanity has always managed to tap new sources and improve the efficiency of oil production. Which of these arguments do you find more persuasive? Explain, citing from the viewpoints.

Chapter 2

1. Dennis Pirages and Theresa DeGeest contend that globalization threatens world health. Richard G.A. Feachem claims that globalization promotes world health. To support their claim, Pirages and DeGeest point to the ongoing process of globalization, the movement of people and goods. Feachem supports his position by pointing to the end goal of globalization, promoting economic growth. Do these different points of reference make one argument more persuasive than the other? Explain.

2. Jeffrey M. Smith claims that genetically modified (GM) food exposes those who eat it to unknown dangers. Gregory Conko and C.S. Prakash claim that such fears are unwarranted. Are you convinced by Conko and Prakash's assurances of GM food safety, or do you join Smith in his concern? What in the authors' texts led you to your conclusion?

Chapter 3

1. Authors in this chapter who dispute that humanity's future is threatened by the human impact on the environment argue that such claims are based on flawed evidence. What kind of evidence do you think would be sufficient to prove to these authors that the threats are serious? Explain, citing from the texts.

2. Mark Lynas claims that global warming is a serious threat to humanity's future. Myron Ebell argues that this claim is misleading. Both authors cite evidence to support their viewpoints, but each cites a different type of evidence. While Ebell cites statistics, Lynas cites personal observations. Which type of evidence do you find more persuasive, and why?

3. Danielle Nierenberg and Mia MacDonald contend that the world's resources cannot sustain an ever-growing human population. They claim that promoting reproductive choice for women and reducing consumption is necessary to meet humanity's needs in the future. Ronald Bailey maintains that despite dire predictions, human ingenuity has always met the challenges of overpopulation in the past and will do so in the future. Do you think relying on human ingenuity alone is sufficient to ensure that the needs of the world's growing population will be met, or do you think the practices recommended by Nierenberg and MacDonald will also be necessary? Explain, citing from the viewpoints.

Chapter 4

1. Bruce R. Scott argues that the income gap between rich and poor nations is growing. Indur M. Goklany asserts that well-being, not gross income, is the better measure of humanity's progress and that well-being is improving. Which argument do you find more persuasive? Explain, citing from the viewpoints.

2. George W. Bush contends that weapons of mass destruction are a serious threat, especially in the hands of terrorists and outlaw regimes. Ivan Eland claims that the threat is exaggerated. Both cite evidence to support their claims. Which author's evidence do you find more persuasive? Why?

3. Of all the concerns about the future of the global community explored in this chapter, which do you think poses the most serious threat? What evidence in the viewpoint(s) led you to this conclusion?

Organizations to Contact

Alliance for BioIntegrity
2040 Pearl Ln., Fairfield, IA 52556
(641) 472-5554
e-mail: info@biointegrity.org • Web site: www.bio-integrity.org

The Alliance for BioIntegrity is a nonprofit organization that opposes the use of genetic engineering in agriculture and works to educate the public about the dangers of genetically modified foods. Position papers that argue against genetic engineering from legal, religious, and scientific perspectives—including "Why Concerns about Health Risks of Genetically Engineered Food Are Scientifically Justified"—are available on its Web site.

Biotechnology Industry Organization (BIO)
1225 Eye St. NW, Suite 400, Washington, DC 20005
(202) 962-9200 • fax: (202) 962-9201
e-mail: biomember@bio.org • Web site: www.bio.org

BIO represents biotechnology companies, academic institutions, state biotechnology centers, and related organizations that support the use of biotechnology in improving health care, agriculture, efforts to clean up the environment, and other fields. BIO works to educate the public about biotechnology and to respond to concerns about the safety of genetic engineering and other technologies. It publishes *Bioethics: Facing the Future Responsibly* and an introductory guide to biotechnology, which are available on its Web site.

Bluewater Network
311 California St., Suite 510, San Francisco, CA 94104
(415) 544-0790 • fax: (415) 544-0796
e-mail: bluewater@bluewaternetwork.org
Web site: www.bluewaternetwork.org

The Bluewater Network promotes policy changes in government and industry to reduce dependence on fossil fuels and eradicate other root causes of air and water pollution, global warming, and habitat destruction. On its Web site the Bluewater Network publishes fact sheets and articles on global warming, including "Clean Transportation Can Curtail Global Warming."

Cato Institute
1000 Massachusetts Ave. NW, Washington, DC 20001-5403
(202) 842-0200 • fax: (202) 842-3490
e-mail: cato@cato.org • Web site: www.cato.org

The institute is a nonpartisan public policy research foundation dedicated to limiting the role of government and protecting individual liberties. It publishes the quarterly magazine *Regulation*, the bimonthly *Cato Policy Report*, and numerous policy papers and articles on global warming, energy, the environment, and globalization, including "Global Warming: The Origin and Nature of the Alleged Scientific Consensus," "Sustainable Development: A Dubious Solution in Search of a Problem," "No Matter What, the Oil Will Flow," and "The Blessings and Challenges of Globalization," which are available on its Web site.

Center for Bioethics and Human Dignity (CBHD)
2065 Half Day Rd., Bannockburn, IL 60015
(847) 317-8180 • fax: (847) 317-8153
e-mail: info@cbhd.org • Web site: www.cbhd.org

CBHD is an international education center whose purpose is to bring Christian perspectives to bear on contemporary bioethical challenges facing society. Its publications address genetic technologies as well as other topics, such as euthanasia and abortion. It publishes the book *Cutting-Edge Bioethics* and the audio CD *The Challenges and Opportunities of Genetic Intervention*. The article "Biotechnology's Brave New World" is available on its Web site.

Competitive Enterprise Institute (CEI)
1001 Connecticut Ave. NW, Suite 1250, Washington, DC 20036
(202) 331-1010 • fax: (202) 331-0640
e-mail: info@cei.org • Web site: www.cei.org

CEI is a nonprofit public policy organization dedicated to advancing the principles of free enterprise and limited government. It believes that individuals are best helped not by government intervention, but by making their own choices in a free marketplace. CEI's publications include the monthly newsletter *Monthly Planet* and articles, including "The Winds of Global Change: Which Way Are They Blowing?" and "The Triumph of Democratic Capitalism: The Threat of Global Governance," which are available on its Web site.

Earth Island Institute
300 Broadway, Suite 28, San Francisco, CA 94133
(415) 788-3666 • fax: (415) 788-7324
e-mail: earthisland@earthisland.org
Web site: www.earthisland.org

Earth Island Institute's work addresses environmental issues and their relation to such concerns as human rights and economic development in the Third World. The institute's publications include the quarterly *Earth Island Journal*. The articles "Bucking the Corporate Future" and "In Favor of a New Protectionism," are available on its Web site.

Friends of the Earth
1717 Massachusetts Ave. NW, Suite 600, Washington, DC 20036-2002
(877) 843-8687 • fax: (202) 783-0444
e-mail: foe@foe.org • Web site: www.foe.org

Friends of the Earth is a national advocacy organization dedicated to protecting the planet from environmental degradation; preserving biological, cultural, and ethnic diversity; and empowering citizens to have an influential voice in decisions affecting the quality of their environment. It publishes the quarterly *Friends of the Earth Newsmagazine*, recent and archived issues of which are available on its Web site.

Global Policy Forum (GPF)
777 UN Plaza, Suite 7G, New York, NY 10017
(212) 557-3161 • fax: (212) 557-3165
e-mail: globalpolicy@globalpolicy.org
Web site: www.globalpolicy.org

GPF monitors policy making at the United Nations, promotes accountability for global decisions, educates and mobilizes citizen participation, and advocates on vital issues of international peace and justice. The forum publishes policy papers and the *GPF Newsletter*. On its Web site GPF provides internal links on topics such as globalization, the future of state sovereignty, and international justice.

The Heritage Foundation
214 Massachusetts Ave. NE, Washington, DC 20002
(202) 546-4400 • fax: (202) 546-0904
e-mail: info@heritage.org • Web site: www heritage.org

The Heritage Foundation is a conservative think tank that supports the principles of free enterprise and limited government. Its many publications include the quarterly magazine *Policy Review* and the occasional papers series *Heritage Talking Points*. On its Web site the foundation includes articles on many issues concerning humanity's future, including globalization.

Human Rights Watch
350 Fifth Ave., New York, NY 10118-3299
(212) 290-4700
e-mail: hrwnyc@hrw.org • Web site: www.hrw.org

Human Rights Watch is an activist organization dedicated to protecting the human rights of people around the world. It investigates and exposes human rights violations and holds abusers accountable. On its Web site Human Rights Watch provides links to subtopics on issues concerning humanity's future, including arms; economic, social, and cultural rights; AIDS; and international justice.

Institute for Alternative Futures (IAF)
100 N. Pitt St., Suite 235, Alexandria, VA 22314
(703) 684-5880 • fax: (703) 684-0640
Web site: www.altfutures.com

IAF consults with and provides speakers to various organizations concerned with health futures, information futures, and business and community futures. On its Web site the institute provides a list of its publications on the environment, anticipatory democracy, and health.

International Forum on Globalization (IFG)
1009 General Kennedy Ave., Suite 2, San Francisco, CA 94129
(415) 561-7650 • fax: (415) 561-7651
e-mail: ifg@ifg.org • Web site: www.ifg.org

IFG is a coalition of nongovernmental organizations that educates activists, policy makers, and the media about the effects of economic globalization. It publishes several books and reports on globalization, including *Intrinsic Consequences of Economic Globalization on the Environment* and *Alternatives to Economic Globalization*.

International Monetary Fund (IMF)
700 Nineteenth St. NW, Washington, DC 20431
(202) 623-7000 • fax: (202) 623-4661
e-mail: publicaffairs@imf.org • Web site: www.imf.org

The IMF is an international organization of 184 member countries. It was established to promote international monetary cooperation, exchange stability, and orderly exchange arrangements. IMF fosters economic growth and high levels of employment and provides temporary financial assistance to countries. It publishes the quarterly *Finance & Development* and reports on its activities, including the quarterly *Global Financial Stability Report*, recent issues of which are available on its Web site along with data on IMF finances and individual country reports.

Organic Consumers Association (OCA)
6101 Cliff Estate Rd., Little Marais, MN 55614
(218) 226-4164 • fax: (218) 353-7652
Web site: www.organicconsumers.org

OCA promotes food safety, organic farming, and sustainable agriculture practices. It provides information on the hazards of genetically engineered food, irradiated food, food grown with toxic sludge fertilizer, mad cow disease, rBGH in milk, and other issues and organizes boycotts and protests around these issues. It publishes *BioDemocracy News* and its Web site includes many fact sheets and articles on genetically modified foods.

Physicians for Social Responsibility (PSR)
1875 Connecticut Ave. NW, Suite 1012, Washington, DC 20009
(202) 667-4260 • fax: (202) 667-4201
e-mail: psrnatl@psr.org • Web site: www.psr.org

Founded in 1961, PSR documented the presence of strontium-90 —a highly radioactive waste product of atmospheric nuclear testing—in American children's teeth. This finding led rapidly to the Limited Nuclear Test Ban treaty that ended above-ground nuclear explosions by the superpowers. PSR's mission is to address public health threats that affect people in the United States and around the world. The PSR Web site publishes fact sheets and article excerpts, including "Healthy Fish, Healthy Families" and "Asthma and the Role of Air Pollution."

Resources for the Future (RFF)
1616 P St. NW, Washington, DC 20036
(202) 328-5000 • fax: (202) 939-3460
Web site: www.rff.org

RFF is a nonprofit research organization concerned with the conservation, management, and development of natural resources. Its research areas include forestry economics, land use and planning, surface and groundwater resources, energy, and environmental quality. On its Web site RFF publishes congressional testimony, discussion papers, reports, and recent issues of its quarterly magazine, *Resources.*

United Nations Development Programme (UNDP)
1 United Nations Plaza, New York, NY 10017
(212) 906-5315 • fax: (212) 906-5364
Web site: www.undp.org

UNDP funds six thousand projects in more than 150 developing countries and territories. It works with governments, UN agencies, and nongovernmental organizations to enhance self-reliance and promote sustainable human development. Its priorities include improving living standards, protecting the environment, and applying technology to meet human needs. UNDP's publications include the weekly newsletter *UNDP Flash*, the human development magazine *Choices*, and the annual *UNDP Human Development Report*. On its Web site UNDP publishes the *Millennium Development Goals*, its annual report, regional data and analysis, speeches and statements, and recent issues of its publications.

World Bank
1818 H St. NW, Washington, DC 20433
(202) 477-1234 • fax: (202) 577-0565
Web site: www.worldbank.org

Formally known as the International Bank for Reconstruction and Development, the World Bank seeks to reduce poverty and improve the standards of living of poor people around the world. It promotes sustainable growth and investments in developing countries through loans, technical assistance, and policy guidance. The World Bank publishes books on global issues, including *Global Economic Prospects 2005: Trade, Regionalism, and Development*; *Privatization in Latin America: Myths and Reality*; and *Intellectual Property and Development: Lessons from Recent Economic Research*. On its Web site the World Bank provides current development data and programs.

World Future Society
7910 Woodmont Ave., Suite 450, Bethesda, MD 20814
(301) 656-8274 • fax: (301) 951-0394
Web site: www.wfs.org

The society serves as a national clearinghouse for ideas and information about the future, including forecasts, recommendations, and alternative scenarios. These ideas help people to anticipate what may happen in coming years and to distinguish between possible, probable, and desired futures. The society publishes the bimonthly *Futurist* magazine and *Futures Research Quarterly*. On its Web site the society publishes lists of recommended books on issues concerning humanity's future, including energy, the environment, governance, health, and science and technology.

World Trade Organization (WTO)
Centre William Rappard, Rue de Lausanne 154, CH-1211 Geneva 21, Switzerland
(41-22) 739 51 11 • fax: (41-22) 731 42 06
e-mail: enquiries@wto.org • Web site: www.wto.org

WTO is a global international organization that establishes rules dealing with the trade between nations. Two WTO agreements have been negotiated and signed by the bulk of the world's trading nations and ratified in their parliaments. The goal of these agreements is to help producers of goods and services, exporters, and importers conduct their business. WTO publishes trade statistics, research and analysis, studies, reports, and the journal *World Trade Review*. Recent publications are available on the WTO Web site.

World Transhumanist Association
PO Box 128, Willington, CT 06279
860-297-2376 • fax: 860-297-4136
e-mail: secretary@transhumanism.org
Web site: http://transhumanism.org

The World Transhumanist Association is an international non-profit organization that advocates the ethical use of technology to expand human capacities. It supports the development of and access to new technologies that enable people to enhance their minds and their bodies. On its Web site the association publishes fact sheets, opinions, and news concerning human enhancement issues.

Worldwatch Institute
1776 Massachusetts Ave. NW, Washington, DC 20036-1904
(202) 452-1999 • fax: (202) 296-7365
e-mail: worldwatch@worldwatch.org
Web site: www.worldwatch.org

Worldwatch is a research organization that analyzes and calls attention to global problems, including environmental concerns such as the loss of cropland, forests, habitat, species, and water supplies. It compiles the annual *State of the World* anthology and publishes the bimonthly magazine *World Watch* and the World Watch Paper Series, which includes "Home Grown: The Case for Local Food in a Global Market" and "Underfed and Overfed: The Global Epidemic of Malnutrition."

Bibliography

Michael R. Alvarez and Thad E. Hall — *Click and Vote: The Future of Internet Voting.* Washington, DC: Brookings Institution Press, 2004.

Robin Attfield — *Environmental Ethics: An Overview for the Twenty-First Century.* Malden, MA: Polity Press, 2003.

Harold W. Baillie and Timothy K. Casey, eds. — *Is Human Nature Obsolete? Genetics, Bioengineering, and the Future of the Human Condition.* Cambridge, MA: MIT Press, 2005.

Lourdes Beneria and Savitri Bisnath, eds. — *Global Tensions: Challenges and Opportunities in the World Economy.* New York: Routledge, 2004.

Jagdish N. Bhagwati — *In Defense of Globalization.* New York: Oxford University Press, 2004.

Alan Bryman — *The Disneyization of Society.* Thousand Oaks, CA: Sage, 2004.

Zbigniew Brzezinski — *The Choice: Global Domination or Global Leadership.* New York: Basic Books, 2004.

Fritjof Capra — *The Hidden Connections: A Science for Sustainable Living.* New York: Doubleday, 2002.

John Cavanagh and Jerry Mander, eds. — *Alternatives to Economic Globalization: A Better World Is Possible.* San Francisco: Berrett-Koehler, 2004.

Audrey R. Chapman and Mark S. Frankel, eds. — *Designing Our Descendants: The Promises and Perils of Genetic Modifications.* Baltimore: Johns Hopkins University Press, 2003.

Noam Chomsky — *Government in the Future.* New York: Seven Stories, 2005.

Amy Chua — *World on Fire: How Exporting Free Market Democracy Breeds Ethnic Hatred and Global Instability.* New York: Doubleday, 2003.

Brian Cooney — *Posthumanity: Thinking Philosophically About the Future.* Lanham, MD: Rowman & Littlefield, 2004.

Jonathan Friedman and Shalini Randeria, eds. — *Worlds on the Move: Globalization, Migration, and Cultural Security.* New York: Palgrave Macmillan, 2004.

Francis Fukuyama — *Our Posthuman Future: Consequences of the Biotechnology Revolution.* New York: Farrar, Straus and Giroux, 2002.

Anthony Giddens — *Runaway World: How Globalization Is Reshaping Our Lives.* New York: Routledge, 2000.

Robert Guest — *The Shackled Continent: Africa's Past, Present, and Future.* London: Macmillan, 2004.

Michael Krepon — *Cooperative Threat Reduction, Missile Defense, and the Nuclear Future.* New York: Palgrave Macmillan, 2003.

Anthony F. Lang Jr., Albert C. Pierce, and Joel H. Rosenthal, eds. — *Ethics and the Future of Conflict: Lessons from the 1990s.* Upper Saddle River, NJ: Pearson/Prentice-Hall, 2004.

Michael A. Levi — *The Future of Arms Control.* Washington, DC: Brookings Institution Press, 2005.

William Ross McCluney — *Humanity's Environmental Future: Making Sense in a Troubled World.* Cape Canaveral, FL: Sun-Pine Press, 2004.

Maxwell J. Mehlman — *Wondergenes: Genetic Enhancement and the Future of Society.* Bloomington: Indiana University Press, 2003.

Tom Mertes, ed. — *A Movement of Movements: Is Another World Really Possible?* New York: Verso, 2004.

William M. Mott — *Globalization: People, Perspectives, and Progress.* Westport, CT: Praeger, 2004.

Cynthia Needham and Richard Canning — *Global Disease Eradication: The Race for the Last Child.* Washington, DC: ASM Press, 2003.

Robert Olson and David Rejeski, eds. — *Environmentalism and the Technologies of Tomorrow: Shaping the Next Industrial Revolution.* Washington, DC: Island Press, 2005.

Patrick O'Meara, Howard D. Mehlinger, and Matthew Krain, eds. — *Globalization and the Challenges of the New Century.* Bloomington: Indiana University Press, 2000.

Harry Redner — *Conserving Cultures: Technology, Globalization, and the Future of Local Cultures.* Lanham, MD: Rowman & Littlefield, 2004.

Jeremy Rifkin — *The Hydrogen Economy: The Creation of the Worldwide Energy Web and the Redistribution of Power on Earth.* New York: Tarcher/Putnam, 2003.

Paul Roberts — *The End of Oil: On the Edge of a Perilous New World.* Boston: Houghton Mifflin, 2004.

Joseph J. Romm — *The Hype About Hydrogen: Fact and Fiction in the Race to Save the Climate.* Washington, DC: Island Press, 2004.

Douglas Schuler and Peter Day, eds. — *Shaping the Network Society: The New Role of Civil Society in Cyberspace.* Cambridge, MA: MIT Press, 2004.

Jeffrey M. Smith	*Seeds of Deception: Exposing Industry and Government Lies About the Safety of the Genetically Engineered Foods You're Eating.* Fairfield, IA: Yes Books, 2003.
Donald M. Snow	*National Security for a New Era: Globalization and Geopolitics.* New York: Pearson/Longman, 2004.
James Gustave Speth	*Red Sky at Morning: America and the Crisis of the Global Environment.* New Haven, CT: Yale University Press, 2004.
James Gustave Speth	*Worlds Apart: Globalization and the Environment.* Washington, DC: Island Press, 2003.
Gregory Stock	*Redesigning Humans: Our Inevitable Genetic Future.* Boston: Houghton Mifflin, 2002.
Kwok Siu Tong and Chan Sin-wai, eds.	*Culture and Humanity in the New Millennium: The Future of Human Values.* Hong Kong: Chinese University Press, 2002.
Joe Trippi	*The Revolution Will Not Be Televised: Democracy, the Internet and the Overthrow of Everything.* New York: ReganBooks, 2004.
Peter Ulmschneider	*Intelligent Life in the Universe: From Common Origins to the Future of Humanity.* New York: Springer Verlag, 2003.
Felicia Wu	*The Future of Genetically Modified Crops: Lessons from the Green Revolution.* Santa Monica, CA: Rand Science and Technology, 2004.

Web Sites

Betterhumans, www.betterhumans.com. Betterhumans is an online journal that conducts Web forums and publishes news, articles, and editorials on issues concerning humanity's future, including genetic engineering, human and artificial intelligence, longevity, and the exploration of space for human habitation.

Future, www.globalchange.com. Hosted by futurist Patrick Dickson, the Web site publishes speeches and articles by Dickson and other futurists on issues concerning humanity's future such as genetic engineering and the future of economics, health, and the Internet.

Futurist.com, www.futurist.com. Hosted by futurist Glen Hiemstra, the Web site includes news and articles on future trends and issues concerning humanity's future, including "Techno Babble," "Powering the Future," and "The Population Boom Ends with a Whimper!"

Nick Bostrom's Home Page, www.nickbostrom.com. Hosted by Oxford University philosophy professor Nick Bostrom, chair of the World Transhumanist Association, the Web site publishes articles on issues concerning humanity's future, including artificial intelligence, bioethics, human enhancement, and the future of human evolution.

Index